LICK THE BOWL
GOOD

LICK THE BOWL GOOD

Classic Home-Style Desserts with a Twist

Monica Holland

SKYHORSE PUBLISHING

Skyhorse Publishing books may be purchased in bulk at special discounts for sales promotion, corporate gifts, fund-raising, or educational purposes. Special editions can also be created to specifications. For details, contact the Special Sales Department, Skyhorse Publishing, 307 West 36th Street, 11th Floor, New York, NY 10018 or info@skyhorsepublishing.com.

Skyhorse® and Skyhorse Publishing® are registered trademarks of Skyhorse Publishing, Inc. ®, a Delaware corporation.

www.skyhorsepublishing.com

10 9 8 7 6 5 4 3 2

Library of Congress Cataloging-in-Publication Data is on file.

ISBN: 978-1-62636-038-9

Printed in China

For my boys Sam, Jack, and Hayden.
I love you to the moon and back.

TABLE OF CONTENTS

INTRODUCTION: MY JOURNEY

Back in the day, we didn't eat dessert on a regular basis and when we did, it was usually something store bought like Little Debbie snacks, or for a special treat we'd go to Dairy Queen and get a dip cone or a Blizzard. Most of the time if we wanted something sweet, my brother and I would just walk to the corner store and buy a piece of gum or Laffy Taffy for a nickel. That was also when gasoline was 99¢ a gallon! I don't think we'll ever see that again.

Every so often my aunt Melinda would make a cake, usually from a mix. She is five years older than me, and she's always felt more like an older sister than an aunt. I would sit in my grandma's tiny kitchen at the round, wooden table for four and watch her bake. We used the kitchen table as our work surface because counter space was limited and my grandma was often in the kitchen whipping up hearty meals to feed all of us. To this day, she still rolls out homemade flour tortillas at that table. A fresh homemade tortilla hot off the comal with a pat of butter is one of the best snacks you'll ever have. I always wanted to help my aunt because I thought that measuring out ingredients, cracking eggs, and stirring thick sweet batter looked like so much fun. But when I did profess my desire for helping, I got stuck doing the chore *nobody* wants to do—greasing the pans. We couldn't afford to buy nonstick baking spray, so we used what we had on hand, which was shortening and flour. I hated sticking my fingers in that white stuff and smearing it into the pans. It took forever to wash off my hands, and then the flour dust got all over me and the kitchen, but I knew if I wanted to help, this is what I had to do. And I did.

My parents divorced when I was very young. On the weekends that we were with my dad, we would sometimes get to sleep over at our older cousin's house. My brother Joseph and my cousin Vince would watch World Wrestling Federation (WWF) wrestling on TV and pretend they were Hulk Hogan and *Macho Man* Randy Savage. On the other side of the house Christina and I would listen to Bon Jovi while she fixed my hair into a side ponytail. I was definitely a child of the '80s. We would also bake cake mixes together, only she let me help mix the ingredients with a hand mixer, and she let me lick the bowl when we were done. That was the best part.

Over time, my intrigue for baking grew until the day I mustered up enough courage to make my first ever recipe from scratch. I had no idea what I would make until I found a huge jar of welfare peanut butter hiding in a cupboard with a recipe on the back. I read the recipe. We had all the ingredients and it seemed simple enough to take on by myself, so I creamed shortening, peanut butter, and sugar together, added a couple eggs, some flour, and baking soda, and I rolled them into balls before baking. Five dozen dough balls and a couple hours later, I had accomplished my goal—a kitchen full of homemade peanut butter cookies. I was ready to share my gift with the world.

Fast forward a few years . . . I have moved away from my grandparents' home and am newly married to my high school sweetheart, Sam. While Sam and I were dating, he'd call me and we'd stay up until the wee hours of the night talking on the phone. Or rather, I'd do all the talking while he listened and munched on frozen chocolate chips. He loves chocolate! One day while flipping through a magazine I found a recipe for double chocolate chewies.

I jotted down the recipe on a yellow Post-it and filed it away to make for him. I did bake those cookies for him, and I'm convinced that's why he fell in love with me. As they say, the way to a man's heart is through his stomach.

Over the years I didn't do as much baking because my mother-in-law, Nonie, would bake chocolate chip pecan cookies and send them over on a regular basis. My mom, Laura, and I experimented with baking fortune cookies, homemade vanilla wafers, and fruit pizzas. Those were tasty successes. I tried my hand at homemade cookies and ice cream once, which was a total disaster. In my mind, I thought the more cookies, the better it would be. I added so many cookies to that ice cream that it was dense and greasy, and the whole thing turned a grayish-brown color. It was horrifying, but we still managed to choke it down.

Sam and I married and bought a house in 2005. By the summer of 2006, I was pregnant with our first son. I had a fairly easy pregnancy. I was tired and hungry all the time and wanted to eat everything I saw on TV, but the weeks seemed to just fly. Then one early morning in August, I awoke with terrible cramping in my abdomen. I wasn't sure what was happening to my body, but I went to the hospital where I later delivered our premature son at seventeen weeks gestation. We were in shock but wanted a family so badly that we got pregnant again right away. In February 2007, just six months after our first son, we lost yet another baby. Our lives were forever changed.

We grieved and mourned the loss of our sons, Sam and Jack. We searched the Internet for answers to our questions, we attended grief counseling, went to two different therapists, shed countless tears, and shared our story at support groups over and over again. At a hospital support group, I met my dear friend, Monica, who encouraged me to start a blog. I encountered so many people with similar stories. I could relate to others, and I felt less alone. It was helpful to write and express my emotions. I didn't write for an audience, I just let my feelings pour out of me like I was writing a journal. It was freeing and I felt like a weight was lifted off my soul. Blogging helped immensely, and then after a few months it became too much for me to bear. All I did was think about babies and getting pregnant. I missed my boys and got lost in a world of sadness. I was consumed by grief.

I needed another outlet, so in the fall of 2007, I started a recipe blog. I didn't know how the new blog would progress, but I knew that I loved baking and sharing recipes, so I dove head-first with my favorite chocolate zucchini bundt cake. The first few months were sketchy, and there were times when I got discouraged, but I finally had something else to focus my energy on. I began to think about what I would make next. I took pictures of the cakes and cupcakes I made, and over time I got better at it. It became a challenge, and I learned so much about the science behind baking, lighting, food photography, and myself. I was learning to accept the new me, and before I knew it, I was happy again.

We continued to try for another baby, and after years of struggling with infertility, I finally got pregnant again with our third son. In September 2011, we welcomed our little blessing, Hayden, into the world. Getting him here was a long difficult journey, but he was worth the wait. Now he's a very curious curly haired toddler who likes to stand on a chair helping me in the kitchen, sampling my creations as he sees fit, and I wouldn't want it any other way.

Through blogging, I've met some pretty incredible people and have made lifelong friends from all over the world. Some I have met in person, some I have only communicated with through mail or phone, some I have baked with and cried with, and a few have even shared some of life's greatest moments with me. They are all different, but each one of them holds a special place in my heart. This may sound highly dramatic, but blogging changed my life. It is more than just typing words and posting pictures on a website, it is a fulfilling and rewarding community, and I'm proud to be a part of it. I blog to share my knowledge of baking with others. I bake to express my love and appreciation for those who are most important in my life, my friends, and family.

As for the title of my blog and now this cookbook, I can't help but recall that sweet memory of baking with my cousin in her kitchen. It truly was "lick the bowl good."

BAKING ESSENTIALS: TOOLS OF THE TRADE

Whether you are an avid baker or are just starting out, having a well equipped kitchen not only makes baking easier it will ensure better results. Here is a list of equipment and kitchen tools that will allow you to make any of the recipes in this book.

Oven Thermometer: One of the most important and least expensive gadgets you can have in the kitchen is an oven thermometer. If you bake often, it is imperative to know how your oven functions. Many ovens run a few degrees cooler or warmer then you think. Having an oven thermometer will ensure that your oven is up to correct temperature before baking. If your oven is off, you can make adjustments accordingly without having to sacrifice the cake you've worked so hard to bake.

Pans: Having an array of metal pans will allow you to bake many types of cakes, breads, cupcakes and bars. You don't need to have multiples of everything, but if you bake lots of cupcakes or muffins, it comes in handy to have more than one cupcake tin. My preference for baking is high-quality aluminum pans. Darker metal pans conduct heat a little differently and can cause food to brown more quickly.

Besides my metal cake baking pans, I use my 8-inch and 9x13-inch glass and stoneware dishes the most. They are the perfect size for bars, brownies, coffee cakes, etc. Cookie sheets and rimmed baking sheets are multi-purpose pans. Not only can you use them to bake cookies on, you can use them underneath pies to catch drips and they can be used as trays.

The only specialty pans that are required in this book are a large capacity Bundt pan, a tart pan with a removable bottom, and a springform pan. You don't need to make a special purchase for these unless you plan to make cheesecakes, tarts, and Bundt cakes on a regular basis.

Electric Hand Mixer/ Stand Mixer: All the recipes in this book can be made with an inexpensive electric hand mixer. I prefer to use a hand mixer when possible but having a stand mixer does make the process easier especially when you're working with large quantities of batter or cookie dough. Ultimately, it's all a matter of preference.

Food Processor: A food processor is not a piece of equipment I use often, but it is invaluable when making pie crust or fruit puree. It really does speed up the process and gets the job done in seconds with minimal effort.

Kitchen Scale: Many bakers prefer to use kitchen scales to weigh ingredients to get the exact amounts of ingredients for baking. For testing purposes, all the recipes in this book were tested by volume not weight. As long as you use the "scoop and level" method for measuring out ingredients such as flour and sugar, you will have success. Still, the kitchen scale is convenient for weighing items such as chocolate.

Mixing Bowls: You will need a full set of mixing bowls. Tempered glass, stain resistant plastic, and ceramic bowls are all perfectly fine. Larger bowls will allow you to mix batters and doughs while the smaller bowls are great for holding other ingredients. A few recipes call for using several mixing bowls at the same time. Having multiple bowls allows you to continue on with the recipe without having to stop to wash bowls for another use. If you like to set all your ingredients out into bowls before baking— called *mise en place*—several small bowls will come in handy.

Measuring Cups and Spoons: There are two different kinds of measuring cups—those for dry ingredients and those for liquid. You will need a full set (1/4 cup, 1/2 cup, 1/3 cup and 1 cup) of dry measuring cups. These can be either metal or plastic but avoid anything made of ceramic as they can chip or break. One good quality set should last you a lifetime.

Liquid measuring cups are made of plastic and tempered glass and have a spout and a handle. They are often measured in ounces and cups and will have the lines detailed on the cups. You will need a 1 cup, 2 cup and a 4 cup measuring cup.

Measuring spoons are ideal for measuring out smaller quantities such as baking soda or salt. When you see a measurement for a teaspoon, do not go to your silverware and pull out a long spoon that you use to stir your iced tea with. For proper measurements you need a full set (1/8 tsp, 1/4 tsp, 1/2 tsp, 1 tsp, 1 Tablespoon) of metal or plastic spoons.

Rubber Spatulas and Silicone Scrapers: These are the most used tools in my kitchen. I have several colors and sizes and use them to cook and bake with. They are heat proof up to high temperatures and will not melt in your pan. When choosing a spatula, choose ones that fit comfortably in your hand. There are different styles and some have silicone handles, metal handles or wooden handles. Keep in mind that wood cannot go in the dishwasher, and metal conducts heat when selecting the spatula that's right for you. Whichever spatulas you choose, they will help you get the job done. They can stir, scoop, fold and scrape the bowl clean.

Whisks: A few different sizes and styles of whisks will come in handy when making the recipes in this book. I use sturdy metal rust-proof balloon whisks for stirring dry ingredients together or for beating thin batters. A balloon whisk is also great for whipping cream by hand.

I also use sauce whisks, which have a flat bottom, for combining liquids or making sauces in a saucepan. They are also great for cooked custards where you need to constantly whisk so the custard doesn't stick to the pan.

Metal Sieve: A metal sieve is a multi-purpose tool in the kitchen. It can be used to sift dry ingredients or to remove lumps from powdered sugar or cocoa. You can use a sieve to strain a fruit puree if you want a seedless mixture. You can press cooked custards and pudding through them to ensure there aren't any lumps. You can also use them as a strainer for rinsing berries or for dusting powdered sugar over baked goods.

Microplane Zester: If you use a lot of citrus in your baking or cooking, I highly recommend getting a Microplane zester. Originally, these were used as a wood rasp but they're perfect for removing just the outer, brightly colored skin of citrus. All the oils are in the outer layer and that's where all the concentrated flavor lies. Adding zest to a recipe gives it so much flavor. The zester is also great for grating chocolate, and other savory items such as garlic and hard cheeses.

Citrus Reamer: When a recipe calls for citrus juice such as lemon, lime or orange, it is ideal to use freshly squeezed juice and not juice from concentrate or bottled juice. To get the maximum amount of juice from your citrus, a reamer helps tremendously.

Pastry Blender: A pastry blender is useful for cutting butter or shortening into dry ingredients. You use a pastry blender when you want to incorporate small bits of fat into a recipe without blending it all together as you would a batter. You can use them for making pie crust dough by hand or for making crumb toppings or biscuits.

Spring-Loaded Cookie Scoops: I use cookie scoops often and not just for cookies. Cookie scoops are just another tool to help measure out batter and doughs. I use them to portion out cupcake and muffin batter to ensure they are the same size. This also helps to ensure that they bake evenly and at the same time, with uniform results. I also use them to portion out fillings and frosting. It's a great tool for portioning out batter for waffles and pancakes as well.

Offset Spatulas: The thin offset metal blade on this spatula makes it ideal for spreading. I use it to spread batters and doughs into the corners of baking dishes. It's also perfect for frosting cupcakes and cakes. Because the blade is offset (at an angle) and flexible it helps to keep your fingers out of whatever you're spreading.

Bench Scraper: This is used to literally scrape and help lift delicate or sticky doughs from your work surface. If you're rolling out pie dough or cookies and the dough has become soft and is sticking to the counter, a bench scraper can help lift it. It can also be used as a cutting tool to score shortbread or cut bars while they're still in the pan.

Cooling Racks: These are essential in baking to allow your hot baked items to cool while allowing air circulation under them. Cooling racks are great for allowing cookies to cool while remaining flat as well as cooling hot cakes in and out of their pans. They can also be used when applying glaze to baked goods by allowing the excess glaze to drip off through the holes without puddling. Consider getting a couple different sizes for different job.

Parchment Paper: This is a non-stick paper that is used for baking. It can be used on cookie sheets to allow cookies to slide right off the paper without sticking and it can be used to line pans when baking cakes. Most often, I use it to line pans when making brownies, blondies, and bars so it's easier to get them out of the pan in one piece after they have cooled.

BAKING ESSENTIALS: INGREDIENTS

It is important to have a well stocked pantry so when the mood strikes you can head to your kitchen and bake just about anything. I don't always have heavy cream or buttermilk on hand, but my pantry is always stocked with the essentials—flour, sugar, baking powder, baking soda, salt and vanilla. While my refrigerator is stocked with butter and eggs. With these few ingredients you can bake many desserts to satisfy your sweet cravings. Below is a rundown of the ingredients you'll find in this book along with some useful information and measuring guidelines.

FLOUR AND OATS

Flour is a finely milled grain most often made from wheat but can also be made from seeds and nuts. Flour provides structure and body and is essential in most baked products.

Flour contains gluten which is a protein. The amount of protein in the flour affects the overall texture of the baked good. Cake flour contains 6-8% protein which will produce a light and tender cake while bread flour contains 12-14% protein and will results in a chewier loaf of bread. Since all-purpose flour contains medium amounts of protein, it can be used for many types of baked goods. All the recipes in this book were made with unbleached all-purpose flour which contains 10-12% protein.

As flour sits, it settles and becomes compacted so it's important to measure correctly to get the accurate amount of flour for your recipe. To measure flour stir it up with a spoon to lighten it up a bit. Scoop the flour into the measuring cup mounding it slightly. Using a straight edge or the back of a butter knife level off the top making it flush with the top of the cup.

Old Fashioned-Oats are a whole grain that have been flattened for quicker cooking. They are different from quick cooking oats, which have been flaked and further processed for even quicker cooking. For use in this book, Quaker old-fashioned rolled oats have been used. They can be found in the cereal aisle of your supermarket.

SUGAR AND SWEETENERS

Sugars add both sweetness and moisture to baked goods and desserts because when it melts it becomes a liquid. Sugar also helps baked goods brown. Most recipes in this book use granulated, light brown or powdered sugar, but occasionally I use honey or molasses as natural sweeteners.

Granulated Sugar is made from sugar cane or beets, appears white in color, and is the most commonly used form of sugar. It comes in the form of very fine granules and is measured out in the same scoop and level manner as flour.

Brown Sugar is made by adding varying amounts of molasses to granulated sugar. There are two types of brown sugar- light and dark. They can be used interchangeably depending on your taste and how strong you want the molasses flavor to be.

To measure brown sugar, scoop the sugar into a dry measuring cup and pack it firmly into the cup. When turned out, the sugar should hold its shape.

Powdered Sugar is also known as confectioners' sugar or 10X sugar. Powdered sugar is the finest of all sugars and is white and powdery. Powdered sugar is often used in icings, frostings, glazes and for decorating because it dissolves so quickly and doesn't have a granular feel to it. It is measured the same as flour and granulated sugar.

Honey is a natural sugar made from bees and varies in color from light golden to dark golden. The color and flavor vary depending on the nectar the bees have gathered. For baking, a mild honey like clover or wildflower honey is best. Not only will honey sweeten your baked goods, it will keep them moist.

To measure honey, use measuring spoons for small amounts or a liquid measuring cup with spout for larger amounts.

Molasses is a thick, dark brown syrup and is a by-product from the sugar refining process. For use in this book, I used unsulphured molasses which is lighter in color and sweeter than darker or blackstrap molasses which contain less sugar and are slightly bitter.

To measure molasses, use measuring spoons for small amounts or a liquid measuring cup with spout for larger amounts.

LEAVENING AGENTS

Baking Powder is a chemical leavener used in baking that causes baked goods to rise when mixed with a liquid by releasing bubbles of carbon dioxide gas into a batter or dough. It is a combination of baking soda (sodium bicarbonate), cream of tartar and cornstarch. Most baking powder is double-acting. That means it reacts twice, once when it is first mixed with a liquid and secondly with heat. For use in this book, aluminum-free baking powder was used. To ensure freshness, replace your baking powder every 6 to 9 months.

Baking Soda or bicarbonate of soda is used in recipes that also calls for other acidic ingredients such as chocolate, citrus, honey, sour cream or buttermilk. The reaction that happens between the baking soda the acidic ingredients and moisture react immediately and cause the mixture to rise so once it's added to the recipe you need to bake it immediately.

Cream Of Tartar is a byproduct of the wine making process that is used in baking powder. It is often added to egg whites to increase their stability and to help increase volume.

DAIRY

Unsalted Butter is typically used in baking because you can control the amount of salt that goes into the recipe. You can use salted butter if you prefer but you may have to adjust the amount of additional salt that is added. Because of the fat content in butter, margarine is not a suitable substitute for baking. Butter also helps you achieve a nice golden color to your baked goods.

To soften butter, set it out at room temperature for 30-45 minutes. To speed up the process, cut the butter into smaller pieces and allow it to come to room temperature. Microwaving butter is not ideal because it overheats and you'll end up with half cold, half melted butter.

To measure butter refer to the markings on the wrapper or use a measuring cup for larger amounts. For the recipes in this book, first quality Grade A unsalted butter was used.

Brown Butter is butter that has been cooked and browned. You start off by melting the butter in a saucepan, as it boils, sputters and foams slightly, the milk solids cook, resulting in brown bits at the bottom of the pan. The butter turns a lovely hue of gold and it smells rich and nutty. You can use it in place of regular butter and can be used in both sweet and savory recipes. Just be careful not to burn the butter or you'll have to start over.

Milk and Cream are a great way to add moisture, flavor and fat to recipes. Both are very versatile and can be added to cakes, biscuits, custards, glazes and frostings. Generally when a recipe calls for milk, you can use whole, 2% or skim but if a recipe calls for cream you should use cream because you need the fat content.

Cream is the fat that rises to the top of whole milk. It contains 36-40% butterfat and is great for making whipped cream. It is slightly different than "whipping cream" that only has 30% butterfat. Heavy cream is the preferred cream of choice for recipes in this book because it is more stable and will hold it's shape better when whipped.

Buttermilk was originally the liquid left over from the butter churning process. Today, store bought buttermilk is thick cultured low-fat milk that has a tangy flavor to it. Buttermilk not only adds flavor but helps tenderize foods. If you can't find buttermilk, sour milk can be substituted.

To make sour milk: In a 1 cup measuring cup, place 1 Tablespoon of fresh lemon juice or vinegar. Pour regular milk up to the 1 cup line then stir. Allow mixture to sit for 5 minutes before using. Makes 1 cup.

Cream Cheese comes in many forms, from flavored and sweetened, to whipped and low fat. By adding flavors and or removing fat, the texture changes. For consistency, the recipes in this book use plain full fat cream cheese.

Measure and soften cream cheese the same way you would butter by allowing it to sit at room temperature before using. Properly softened cream cheese is key to a successful recipe; otherwise you may end up with a lumpy mixture. Generally, when you have a recipe that calls for cream cheese, you begin by blending the cream cheese in a bowl with a mixer until creamy before adding any additional ingredients. This will also help to ensure that the mixture is well mixed and lump free.

Mascarpone Cheese is an Italian cheese made of milk and cream and has a higher fat content than cream cheese. It is rich and spreadable but can be somewhat bland in taste so it is often used in recipes with bold flavorings rather than just eating it by itself.

Sour Cream is cream that has been fermented with lactic acid cultures that yields a creamy, thick, tangy product. It can be used as a condiment, in baking cakes as well as making frosting and is also used in cooking. Sour cream adds great flavor and moisture to baked goods.

In a pinch, plain Greek yogurt is a great substitute for sour cream in cake recipes.

Sweetened Condensed Milk is a sweet and sticky dairy product sold in cans in the baking aisle. It is prepared by cooking down a mixture of milk and sugar and removing about half of the water content until you're left with a thick concentrated product. Sweetened condensed milk is a key ingredient in key lime pie and should not be confused with evaporated milk which is not sweetened.

Eggs are essential in baking. They provide structure, color, flavor and richness in baked goods and desserts. They can also be used as thickeners and leaveners and can help a cake rise by incorporating air into the batter. Depending on the recipe, you may need the whole egg, eggs whites or egg yolks.

It is easier to separate the egg whites from egg yolks while they are still cold, but you will get more volume from whipped egg whites (meringue) when they are at room temperature. If you accidentally break a yolk into your egg whites, you will need to start over with another egg. The fat content in the yolk will prevent the egg whites from whipping properly and you won't get a proper rise.

For the recipes in this book, large Grade A chicken eggs were used.

CHOCOLATE

Chocolate Chips are a great way to add bits of chocolate throughout a recipe and are great for melting and using in ganache, glazes and frostings.

Semisweet chocolate has always been my chocolate of choice because it isn't too sweet or too bitter. Be sure to look for chocolate that is labeled as "chocolate" not "chocolate flavor" as that is generally artificially flavored. Real chocolate will often have a percentage on the package with the amount of cacao that the product contains. I like to stick to chocolate in the 60% cacao range for baking unless a recipe specifically calls for unsweetened chocolate.

For the recipes in this book, Guittard semisweet chocolate chips were used. Purchase the best quality chocolate you can afford.

Chocolate is measured weight or volume. 6 ounces chocolate chips = 1 cup

Cocoa Powder is what remains from cocoa beans after most of the cocoa butter has been removed. There are two main types of cocoa powder— natural cocoa and Dutch-process cocoa.

With Dutch cocoa, the cocoa beans are soaked in an alkaline solution before drying and grinding them into powder. This process makes the overall product less acidic and darker in color. It also gives the cocoa a deeper chocolate flavor and is less bitter than natural cocoa.

Natural cocoa is untreated and is naturally lighter in color and slightly more bitter than Dutch process cocoa. Because Dutch cocoa is less acidic than natural cocoa, it is often used in recipes that call for baking powder, whereas natural cocoa powder is used in conjunction with baking soda.

If you're unsure what kind of cocoa to use or purchase, choose the brand with the flavor and price point you are comfortable with. Dutch process cocoa is more expensive and not as readily available as natural cocoa.

For the recipes in this book, Hershey's unsweetened natural cocoa powder was used.

FLAVORINGS AND EXTRACTS

Vanilla is probably the most common flavoring component added to desserts and baked goods. Vanilla seems to be a universal flavor that everyone loves and it helps add depth to whatever it is you're making. Even if a recipe doesn't call for vanilla extract, I often add it anyway.

There are different products that can be made from vanilla but it all starts with the vanilla bean pod which comes from an orchid flower.

The actual vanilla pod is full of thousands of tiny blacks seeds that are full of fragrant flavor. It is a more concentrated flavor and is used in steeping in liquids and creams as well as scraping out the seeds and adding them to ice cream, custards, and baked goods. Once the seeds have been scraped out, the pods still hold flavor and can be used to flavor sugar or other liquids.

The most common form of vanilla is vanilla extract, which is made by taking a mixture of alcohol and water and soaking vanilla beans in the solution until it turns dark and aromatic.

The flavor of vanilla will vary depending on the region in which it was grown. Be sure when purchasing vanilla extract that you select Pure Vanilla Extract not Vanillin or Clear Vanilla which are both artificially flavored.

My preference has always been to use Pure Mexican Vanilla Extract but use what you are familiar with.

Extracts are a great way to add flavor to many baked goods. They are generally concentrated flavors and a little goes a long way. Almond extract, in particular, pairs well with stone fruits such as cherries, peaches, plums and apricots. Be sure when purchasing extracts that you avoid anything with the word "Imitation" on the package.

Citrus is a great way to add flavor and brighten a recipe. The fresh juice from oranges, lemons, and limes can add sweetness and/or tartness to a recipe, while the outer colored skin, called the zest, imparts a more concentrated citrus flavor. Just be sure when adding zest to a recipe that you avoid the inner white part, called the pith, because it is bitter. When selecting citrus for zesting choose brightly colored, smooth skin with little to no blemishes.

Coffee and Espresso Powder added to a recipe can intensify the flavor of chocolate. I often use hot brewed coffee in place of water in chocolate cake recipes because it makes the finished product taste deeper and richer and more well rounded, without actually tasting like coffee. Espresso powder has the same affect in brownie or cookie recipes where adding liquid may not be an option.

Liquors and Liqueurs are similar to extracts in that they are flavored alcohols. However when adding liquors and liqueurs to a recipe, you often use a bit more because their flavors aren't as concentrated. In recipes that are baked, the alcohol content dissipates in the oven, but the flavor still remains.

If you're curious about trying different spirits in baking, consider purchasing sample sizes from the liquor store. They often sell tiny little bottles for just a few dollars each and since most recipes only call for a few Tablespoons at most, you're not wasting much money if you happen to not like the flavor.

Nuts are a wonderful addition to baked goods because they lend flavor, texture and nutritional value to whatever they're added to. They are also naturally high in fat which causes them to turn rancid quickly. Be sure to buy fresh nuts and store them in airtight containers. They will keep for several months in the freezer.

Toasting will release the natural oils and bring out the flavor in nuts. Spread nuts on a baking sheet and toast in a 350 degree oven for 8-15 minutes until nuts are uniformly golden and fragrant.

Spices can add warmth, earthiness and dimension to baked goods. Be sure to buy fresh, richly colored spices with a pleasant aroma. If they're old or are lacking in flavor or aroma, discard them and buy fresh. When possible, buy whole spices such as nutmeg and grind them as needed. Store spices away from heat, moisture and sunlight to preserve their flavor.

Salt is essential in baking. You might wonder why you would add salt to sweet desserts, but the answer is simple. Salt brings out the flavor in whatever you are making. It is the key to perking up flavors and providing balance.

I bake with both Iodized table salt and Kosher salt. Table salt is a finer in texture and will dissolve rather quickly, while kosher salt is more coarse. If you intend to use kosher salt, be sure to add it to recipes that contain a lot of liquid so it dissolves properly.

SHORTENING AND OIL

These are often used in baking in place of butter because they not only add moisture to recipes they offer a neutral flavor. Shortening is used in making flaky pie crusts and biscuits. It is also used in frostings because it produces a more stable product that is not as delicate as using all butter. Neutral flavored oils such as vegetable or canola oils produce cakes with a lighter, slightly spongy crumb and can often yield a moister cake for a longer period of time than cakes made with all butter. Sometimes, you'll see a recipe that uses both butter and shortening or oil and that is to impart optimal texture and flavor.

THICKENERS

Cornstarch also called corn flour is a very fine white powder made from corn. It is used in recipes for its thickening power in gravies, sauces, custards and pie fillings. But it is often used in baking recipes in conjunction with flour to add structure and increase the tenderness in whatever you're making. Cornstarch is also a key ingredient in cake flour, which is why so many bakers prefer it to all-purpose flour for yielding tender cakes.

Unflavored Powdered Gelatin is a thickener that is activated by first dissolving the powder in cold water. Once heated, the dissolved gelatin forms a gel-like substance that will thicken and stiffen the mixture it is added to but it needs to time to chill and set up properly. Gelatin is often used to add body and substance to creams, mousses and in this book, panna cotta, which is a cooked cream dessert.

GETTING STARTED: HOW TO USE THIS BOOK

I am a detail-oriented person. I like to be thorough, yet I try to make things as simple as possible. I've done that here in this book. Some of the recipes may seem long, but I've done my best to break them down into manageable steps.

I've heard people say that they are cooks but not bakers. My mom is one of those people. She likes to throw things in a pot, taste as she goes, and comes up with some mighty tasty meals, but no recipe can ever be replicated because she just adds a little bit of this, a little of that, and a pinch of fairy dust when she cooks. That is how you learn to cook. You learn from tasting and trying new flavor combinations and techniques, and you learn what doesn't work for you. But baking is a little different.

I strongly believe if you can read and follow directions, you can bake. Before making any recipe in this book, read the recipe in it's entirety. Read through the ingredient lists and directions. As you read the instructions in your head think about how you would do each step, whether it's buttering a dish and lining it with parchment paper or whipping cream to top a pie. Play it out in your head as if you were physically in your kitchen doing those things. If you have questions about an ingredient, a kitchen tool, or a technique, refer to the "Baking Essentials" chapters in this book, ask a friend, or look online until you feel comfortable proceeding with the recipe.

Read the ingredient lists, and make sure you have everything you need to make the recipe. There's nothing worse then getting started and realizing you're out of eggs or running low on flour and having to run to the market to replenish your stock. Along with that, make sure if the recipe calls for room temperature ingredients that you take your butter and cream cheese out ahead of time. Waiting on rock-hard butter to warm up is frustrating, and placing it in the microwave usually results in hot spots.

I've included some "Baker's Notes" throughout the book that pertain to the recipes. Scan the pages to see if there is a "Baker's Note", and if there, is read it before you proceed with the recipe. It's no fun to get started on a recipe that you intended to serve for dessert that night only to realize you should have made and chilled a portion of it the night before. Again, read the whole recipe before getting started. You will save yourself a lot of unnecessary frustration in the end.

Baking should be fun and is a learning experience. Don't take it so seriously. I have had many flops and disasters come out of my kitchen, several of which were tossed in the garbage or thrown out for the birds

to eat. It can be frustrating and expensive when you want something to turn out perfectly and it just doesn't work. I have cried over cake before, but you don't need to. These recipes have been tested over and over again, and I've done my best to provide you with correct measurements and techniques, so you will have success with them on your first try. When making a recipe, follow it exactly as written on the first round. If you feel it needs more vanilla or less salt, make those adjustments the next time you make the recipe.

The important thing is to enjoy the experience. Baking can be therapeutic and doesn't need to be stressful. Relax, breathe, and believe in yourself and your abilities. Don't worry about the way your frosting looks on your cake. Don't worry if your cookies aren't as round or flat as they are in the pictures. I have a lot of people tell me that their cakes "aren't as pretty" as mine. As I said before, I am detail oriented and a tad obsessive and will spend an hour frosting a cake just until it looks perfect. I'm kind of funny that way, but I'd much rather have an ugly cookie that tastes good than a cake that is beautiful to look at but is dry. Just like in life, physical beauty is not as important as what's on the inside. Taste trumps looks every time. And if you mess up or burn something, don't give up. Be proud of what you've accomplished and know that you are one step closer to making it better.

As you read through *Lick The Bowl Good*, I sincerely hope that you can feel the heart that I have put into this book. I hope you feel confident and encouraged to try any of these dessert recipes. And lastly, I hope that they become a part of your life, and you're able to build lasting memories around them.

—*Monica Holland*

Chapter 1
CAKES

GRANDMA'S CHOCOLATE CAKE

This was one of the first cakes I ever made as a kid in my grandma's kitchen, and it just happens to be her favorite. I make many cakes, but this one I reserve just for her.

You need:

CHOCOLATE CAKE:
2 cups all-purpose flour
2 cups granulated sugar
¼ cup unsweetened cocoa powder
1 teaspoon baking soda
½ teaspoon salt
2 large eggs
1 cup canola oil
1 cup buttermilk
1 cup hot strong-brewed
    coffee or hot water
1 teaspoon vanilla extract

CHOCOLATE CREAM
CHEESE FROSTING:
8 ounces cream cheese, room
    temperature
1 tablespoon milk
4 cups powdered sugar, sifted
3 ounces unsweetened
    chocolate, melted
1 teaspoon vanilla extract
⅛ teaspoon salt

Preparation:

FOR THE CAKE:
- Preheat oven to 350°F.
- Grease and flour three 8- or 9-inch cake pans. Set aside.
- In a large bowl, combine flour, sugar, cocoa, baking soda, and salt. Whisk the dry ingredients together, then add the eggs, oil, and buttermilk and mix until just combined.
- Carefully add the hot coffee and vanilla and mix. Batter will be thin.
- Pour batter evenly into prepared pans.
- Bake for 30 to 35 minutes or until a toothpick inserted into the center comes out clean.
- Cool in pans for 10 minutes, then turn the warm cakes out onto a rack to cool completely.

FOR THE FROSTING:
- In a large bowl, mix the cream cheese and milk together and beat with an electric mixer until smooth and creamy.
- Gradually blend in sifted powdered sugar until all 4 cups have been incorporated. Scrape down the sides of the bowl as necessary.
- Stir in the melted chocolate, then add vanilla and salt. Continue to beat at medium speed for 2 more minutes until the mixture is light and creamy.

TO ASSEMBLE:
- Place one cake layer on a serving platter, top with half a cup of frosting, and spread it out to the edges. Repeat the process for the second layer, then top with the remaining cake layer. Cover the top and the sides with the remaining frosting.
- Store any leftover cake in the refrigerator, covered.

Baker's note
If you find yourself without buttermilk, you can make your own. In a 1 cup measuring cup, place 1 tablespoon of fresh lemon juice or vinegar. Pour regular milk up to the 1 cup line then stir. Allow mixture to sit for 5 minutes before using. Makes 1 cup.

VANILLA BEAN POUND CAKE

One year, I told my little brother, Aaron, to dream up his perfect birthday cake, and I would make it for him. I was expecting him to come back with some grandiose ideas. Instead, he said he just wanted a vanilla cake. I created this perfectly vanilla pound cake with him in mind.

You need:

2 cups all-purpose flour
1 teaspoon baking powder
¼ teaspoon baking soda
½ teaspoon salt
¾ cup unsalted butter, softened
1½ cups granulated sugar
2 large eggs
1½ teaspoons vanilla extract
½ vanilla bean, split lengthwise with seeds scraped out
¾ cup buttermilk

Preparation:

- Preheat oven to 325°F.
- Grease and flour a 9 × 5-inch loaf pan. Set aside.
- In a medium bowl, combine flour, baking powder, baking soda, and salt. Whisk to combine.
- In a large bowl, using an electric mixer, beat the butter at medium speed until very creamy. Gradually add the sugar and beat until well blended until light and fluffy, about 4 minutes.
- Add the eggs one at a time, beating well after each addition. Scrape down the bowl as necessary. Beat in the vanilla extract and the seeds of the vanilla bean.
- On low speed, gradually add one-third of your flour mixture followed by one-half of the buttermilk. Just as soon as the liquid is absorbed, add another one-third of the flour mixture, then the remaining buttermilk. Add the remaining one-third of the flour mixture, and beat just until combined.
- Scrape the batter into the prepared pan.
- Bake for 75 to 80 minutes or until a toothpick inserted into the center comes out clean.
- Cool in pan for 15 minutes before turning it out onto a rack to cool completely.
- Store at room temperature.

Baker's note

This cake can be made ahead of time and will remain fresh and moist for days, if well wrapped.

CHERRY ALMOND BUNDT CAKE

Rather than adding the sliced almonds into the batter, they are used here to line the pan and form a nutty crust.

You need:

CHERRY ALMOND CAKE:
2 tablespoons unsalted butter, room temperature, for buttering the pan
⅓ cup sliced almonds
1¼ cups unsalted butter, room temperature
1½ cups granulated sugar
4 large eggs
1 teaspoon vanilla extract
1 teaspoon almond extract
¾ cup buttermilk
2¼ cups all-purpose flour
1 tablespoon baking powder
½ teaspoon salt
1-10 ounce jar maraschino cherries, drained and patted dry

ALMOND CREAM:
1 cup heavy cream
¼ cup powdered sugar
½ teaspoon almond extract

Preparation:

FOR THE CAKE:
- Preheat oven to 325°F.
- Thoroughly butter the insides of a Bundt pan. Do not be tempted to use nonstick cooking spray here. Scatter the sliced almonds into the pan and gently press them into the bottom, sides, and center of the pan. Set aside.
- Finely chop the cherries and set aside.
- In a medium bowl, combine the flour, baking powder, and salt. Stir to combine and set aside.
- In a large bowl, cream the butter and sugar until light and fluffy at medium speed. Slowly add the eggs one at a time, taking the time to scrape down the bowl as necessary. Add the vanilla and almond extracts and mix until well combined.
- Add half of the flour mixture to the creamed butter and sugar. Beat just until incorporated, then add all of the buttermilk. Mix until combined, then add the remaining flour mixture. Beat until the flour is just incorporated, scraping down the bowl as necessary.
- Using a spatula, stir the chopped cherries into the batter, making sure they're evenly distributed. Scrape the batter into almond-lined pan.
- Bake for 45 to 55 minutes or until a toothpick inserted into the center comes out clean. Allow cake to cool in pan for 10 minutes before inverting onto a rack to cool completely.

FOR THE ALMOND CREAM:
- In a medium bowl, whip cream, powdered sugar, and almond extract over medium-high speed with a hand mixer. Continue to whip until the mixture has thickened and is creamy and fluffy, but do not over beat or your cream will curdle. Serve well chilled.

IRISH CREAM CAKE

I may not wear green on St. Patrick's Day, but I do make this cake every year.

You need:

CAKE:

⅔ cup all-purpose flour
¼ teaspoon baking powder
⅛ teaspoon baking soda
⅛ teaspoon salt
3 tablespoon unsalted butter, room temperature
½ cup granulated sugar
1 large egg
½ teaspoon vanilla extract
¼ cup Irish cream liqueur
2 tablespoons milk

GLAZE:

2 tablespoons unsalted butter, room temperature
¾ cup powdered sugar
1 tablespoon Irish cream liqueur
1 teaspoon milk
cappuccino chips or chocolate chips for garnish, optional

Preparation:

FOR THE CAKE:

- Preheat oven to 350°F.
- Grease and flour an 8-inch or 9-inch pan and set aside.
- In a small bowl, combine flour, baking powder, baking soda, and salt. Whisk to combine and set aside.
- In a large bowl, cream butter and sugar together until light and fluffy. Add the egg and vanilla extract and beat until combined.
- Mix in half of the flour mixture, followed by the Irish cream and milk. Once the liquid is absorbed, add the remaining flour mixture and mix til well blended. Scrape the batter into prepared pan.
- Bake for 23 to 25 minutes or until a toothpick inserted in the center comes out clean.
- Cool the cake in the pan for 10 minutes before turning it out onto a rack to cool completely.
- Once the cake has cooled, place it on your serving platter and make the glaze.

FOR THE GLAZE:

- In a small bowl, combine butter, powdered sugar, Irish cream, and milk. Whisk together until well blended and pourable.
- Pour the glaze over the cake. While the glaze is still wet, garnish with chocolate chips, if desired. Allow the glaze to set before serving.
- Store at room temperature.

ORANGE POPPY SEED CAKE

A twist on the more common lemon poppy seed cake—this is unmistakably orange.

You need:

CAKE:

1½ cups all-purpose flour
1 tablespoon baking powder
½ teaspoon baking soda
¼ teaspoon salt
3 tablespoons poppy seeds
½ cup plain Greek yogurt or
　　sour cream
2 large eggs
¼ cup fresh orange juice
1 teaspoon vanilla extract
½ cup unsalted butter, room
　　temperature
¾ cup granulated sugar
1 tablespoon finely grated
　　orange zest

GLAZE:

¾ cup powdered sugar
1 teaspoon finely grated
　　orange zest
2 tablespoons fresh
　　orange juice

Preparation:

FOR THE CAKE:

- Preheat oven to 350°F.
- Grease and flour a 9-inch pan and set aside.
- In a small bowl, combine the flour, baking powder, baking soda, salt, and poppy seeds. Whisk to combine.
- In a 2-cup measuring cup, combine yogurt, eggs, orange juice, and vanilla. Whisk the ingredients together until well blended.
- In a large bowl, cream together the butter, sugar, and orange zest until light and fluffy.
- Add one-third of the flour mixture to the creamed butter and sugar. Beat just until incorporated, then add half of the yogurt mixture. Mix until combined, then add one-third more of the flour mixture and the remaining yogurt mixture. Once the liquid had been incorporated, mix in the remaining flour mixture. Beat until the flour is just incorporated, scraping down the bowl as necessary.
- Scrape the batter into the prepared pan.
- Bake for 30 to 35 minutes or until a toothpick inserted into the center comes out clean.
- Cool cake in pan for 10 minutes before turning out onto a rack to cool completely.
- Once the cake has cooled, place it on your serving platter and make the glaze.

FOR THE GLAZE:

- In a small bowl, whisk together the powdered sugar, orange zest, and juice.
- Pour the glaze over the cake. Allow the glaze to set before serving.

FRESH STRAWBERRY CAKE

I've been making this birthday cake for my sister, Samantha, since 2005, and every March she calls me to put in her request for this strawberry-topped showstopper. As long as I'm able, I'll continue to bake this cake for her.

You need:

CAKE:

1½ to 2 cups fresh ripe strawberries
1 tablespoon granulated sugar
2½ cups all-purpose flour
1¼ cup granulated sugar
1-3 ounce box strawberry gelatin
4 teaspoons baking powder
½ teaspoon salt
12 tablespoons unsalted butter, room temperature
½ cup milk
½ teaspoon vanilla
4 large eggs

CREAM CHEESE FROSTING:

1 cup unsalted butter, room temperature
8 ounces cream cheese, room temperature
1 teaspoons vanilla extract
5 cups powdered sugar, sifted

GARNISH:

1 pound fresh strawberries

Preparation:

FOR THE CAKE:

- Preheat oven to 350°F.
- Grease and flour three 8-inch pans and set aside.
- Start by making the strawberry puree. Use the darkest, ripest berries you can find. Rinse and remove the stems and hulls. Place the berries in a food processor or blender with 1 tablespoon of sugar, and blend the fruit until there are no lumps, and the fruit puree is smooth. Measure out ¾ cup to use in the cake. If you have any leftover, refrigerate for another use.
- In a large bowl, combine the flour, sugar, powdered gelatin, baking powder, and salt. Whisk to combine.
- Add the softened butter to the dry ingredients. Mix until the butter is incorporated and soft crumbs form. It will look and feel like sand.
- Add ¾ cup strawberry purée, milk, and vanilla to the crumbly mixture and mix to combine.
- Add the eggs one at a time, mixing well after each addition. Mix until all the ingredients are well incorporated, scraping down the bowl as necessary, but do not overmix the batter.
- Divide the batter evenly between the prepared pans.
- Bake for 22 to 25 minutes or until a toothpick inserted into the center comes out clean.
- Cool cakes in pans for 10 minutes before turning them out onto a rack to cool completely.

FOR THE FROSTING:

- In a large bowl, combine butter and cream cheese and beat with an electric mixer at medium speed until light and creamy.
- Add the vanilla extract and mix until combined. Add the powdered sugar one cup at a time until all the sugar has been incorporated, stopping to scrape down the sides of the bowl, as necessary. Use immediately.

Continued …

FRESH STRAWBERRY CAKE ASSEMBLY

TO ASSEMBLE:

- Place one cake layer on a serving platter, top with ½ to ¾ cup of frosting and spread it out to the edges. Repeat the process for the second layer, then top with the remaining cake layer. Cover the top and the sides with the remaining frosting. You will have enough frosting to pipe a decorative border on the edges of the cake, if you desire.
- Store the frosted cake in the refrigerator for a minimum of 30 minutes to harden and set the frosting.
- Decorate the top of the cake with fresh sliced strawberries just before serving.

TO MAKE THE STRAWBERRY FLOWER:

- Medium sized, blemish-free berries work best for this. Rinse and pat dry your berries, then cut off the green tops.
- Slice the strawberries, lengthwise, about ¼-inch thick. The center slices of the berries will look the best when forming the strawberry design on the cake.
- Starting from the outside, form a circle of berries, with the tips of the strawberries pointing outwards. Repeat this step until you've reached the center of the cake. As the circle becomes tighter, you can just tuck the smaller slices in to fill in any gaps. Place a small upside down berry in the center of the cake to complete the strawberry flower design.

Baker's note
You can make the strawberry puree up to 3 days ahead of time, but don't be tempted to slice the strawberries until just before garnishing the the top of the cake or they'll dry out.

CHOCOLATE ZUCCHINI BUNDT CAKE

This is one of my favorite cakes and the first recipe I ever shared on my blog. I've made this for many family get-togethers and even a few birthdays. The crunchy sugared crust is the best part and because it's loaded with zucchini, it stays moist for several days.

You need:

2 tablespoons unsalted butter, room temperature

2 to 3 tablespoons granulated sugar

⅔ cup unsweetened cocoa powder

2 tablespoon unsalted butter, melted

1 cup canola oil

1 teaspoon vanilla

3 cups all-purpose flour

1½ teaspoon baking powder

1 teaspoon baking soda

1 teaspoon salt

4 large eggs

3 cups granulated sugar

3 cups coarsely grated zucchini, packed

Preparation:

- Preheat oven to 350°F.
- Thoroughly coat the insides of a 15-cup Bundt pan with softened butter. Do not be tempted to use nonstick cooking spray here. Dust the inside of the buttered pan with sugar, and swirl the pan around to coat it thoroughly. Tap out any excess sugar and set pan aside while you make the cake batter.
- In a small bowl, whisk together cocoa, melted butter, oil, and vanilla.
- In a medium bowl, sift together flour, baking powder, baking soda, and salt.
- In a large mixing bowl, beat eggs and slowly add sugar, until thick and light in color.
- Add cocoa mixture to eggs and blend until well combined, then gradually add the flour mixture, being careful not to overmix. Once mixture is well incorporated, add grated zucchini.
- Carefully pour batter into prepared pan.
- Bake for 65 to 70 minutes until toothpick inserted in the center comes out clean.
- Allow cake to cool in the pan for 20 minutes before inverting onto a rack to cool completely.

Baker's note

This makes a large cake, and you need the biggest capacity Bundt pan you can find. Fill your pan no more than three-fourths full. If you have leftover batter, bake cupcakes to avoid overflow in the oven.

BANANA PUDDING CHEESECAKE

I've been making banana pudding desserts for the patriarchs of my family for years. I came up with this over-the-top cheesecake for my father-in-law's seventy-second birthday. He showed his appreciation by devouring several slices.

You need:

COMPONENTS:
vanilla wafer crust
cheesecake filling
vanilla pudding filling
2 to 3 medium bananas
22 vanilla wafers
vanilla whipped cream for
    topping

CRUST:
2 cups vanilla wafer crumbs
    (about 70 wafers)
½ cup unsalted butter, melted

CHEESECAKE:
16 ounces cream cheese,
    room temperature
⅔ cup granulated sugar
1 tablespoon cornstarch
½ teaspoon vanilla extract
1 large egg

PUDDING:
½ cup granulated sugar
⅓ cup cornstarch
¼ teaspoon salt
2 cups milk
3 large egg yolks
1 teaspoon vanilla extract

WHIPPED CREAM:
1 cup heavy cream
¼ cup powdered sugar
1 teaspoon vanilla extract

Preparation:

FOR THE CHEESECAKE:
- Preheat oven to 300°F.
- In a large bowl, beat cream cheese over medium speed until creamy. Slowly add sugar, scraping down the sides of the bowl as necessary. Mix in the cornstarch. Add vanilla and egg and mix until just blended. Scrape down the bowl once more to ensure that everything is evenly incorporated, then beat once more until creamy.
- Pour the batter into the frozen crust.
- Bake for 40 minutes.
- Gently remove the cheesecake from oven to a cooling rack. Allow to cool to room temperature then cover with plastic wrap and chill for at least 2 to 3 hours or overnight.

Baker's note

Do not overbeat the mixture or beat at too high of a speed. Doing so will incorporate too much air into the batter, and your cheesecake will have air bubbles in it. It could crack in the oven, or it will rise and sink, and you'll have a crater in the middle of your cheesecake.

FOR THE CRUST:
- In a medium bowl, stir together vanilla wafer crumbs and butter and press into the bottom and up the sides of a 9-inch springform pan. Press crumbs up the sides about 1¾ inches tall. Once crumbs have been firmly pressed into the pan, place it in the freezer while you prepare the cheesecake filling.

FOR THE PUDDING:
- Place a metal sieve over a medium mixing bowl. Set aside.
- In a saucepan, stir dry ingredients together. Whisk in the egg yolks, then slowly add milk as you continue to whisk the mixture together.
- Heat over medium heat, whisking constantly, until thickened. This happens very quickly (5 to 8 minutes) and gets *very* thick. As soon as the pudding thickens, take it off the heat and whisk vigorously to avoid lumps.
- Push the thickened pudding through a sieve to ensure its completely creamy and free of any lumps.
- Press a piece of plastic wrap directly onto the pudding to avoid forming a skin on the custard. Cool to room temperature and refrigerate for 2 to 3 hours or overnight.

Continued...

BANANA PUDDING CHEESECAKE ASSEMBLY

- Once the cheesecake and pudding is sufficiently chilled, you can begin assembly. Your pudding will be very thick and stiff, almost like mashed potatoes. Don't be worried—it needs to be this thick to hold its shape. Using a balloon whisk, whisk your custard to loosen it up. Keep whisking to remove any lumps.
- Cut your bananas into one-quarter inch slices. Layer the banana slices tightly into a single layer over the cheesecake.
- Spoon half of the pudding over the bananas, gently pressing it into the crevices. Smooth into an even layer.
- Place vanilla wafers in one layer over the pudding, and cover with the remaining pudding. Smooth the top and set aside while you make the vanilla whipped cream.

FOR THE WHIPPED CREAM:

- In a medium bowl, combine all ingredients and beat with an electric mixer over medium speed until thick and creamy and your cream holds stiff peaks, but is not dry.
- Spoon cream over your pudding layer, or pipe rosettes over the pudding in a decorative pattern.
- Chill cheesecake for at least 2 hours then remove the outer ring of the springform pan before serving.
- Serve with fresh banana slices and additional vanilla wafers, if desired.
- Store any leftovers in the refrigerator, well wrapped.

Baker's note

This cheesecake has multiple steps but none of them are difficult. You can break up the process into two days. Prepare the crust, bake the cheesecake, and make the pudding the night before to ensure they are properly chilled, then assemble the cheesecake on the day you need it.

PEACH MELBA BUTTERMILK CAKE

A great way to use up ripened stone fruit or berries, this buttermilk cake is moist and lightly sweetened.

You need:

1½ cups all-purpose flour
1½ teaspoons baking powder
½ teaspoon salt
½ cup unsalted butter, room temperature
1 cup granulated sugar
1 large egg
⅔ cup buttermilk
1 teaspoon vanilla extract
¼ teaspoon almond extract
2 to 3 medium sized ripe peaches, cut into ½-inch thick slices
½ cup fresh raspberries
2 tablespoons granulated sugar

Preparation:

- Preheat oven to 350°F.
- Butter a 9-inch deep dish pie plate and set aside.
- In a medium bowl, sift flour, baking powder, and salt together.
- In a large bowl, cream together butter and 1 cup sugar. Mix on medium-high speed until pale and fluffy.
- Reduce speed to low and mix in egg, buttermilk, vanilla, and almond extracts.
- Gradually mix the flour mixture into the butter mixture, beating until just combined.
- Scrape the batter into the buttered pie plate. Arrange the peaches close together in a single layer on top of batter. Fill in any gaps with the raspberries. Sprinkle 2 tablespoons granulated sugar over the fruit.
- Bake cake 10 minutes at 350°F, then reduce oven temperature to 325°F. Bake until cake is lightly golden brown and the center is firm to the touch, about 60 minutes.
- Cool the cake in the pan on a wire rack. Serve cake with a scoop of vanilla ice cream.

APPLE CAKE WITH CINNAMON BROWN SUGAR GLAZE

A family favorite that gets better by the day.

You need:

APPLE CAKE:

2 eggs
½ cup canola oil
1 teaspoon vanilla extract
1½ cups all-purpose flour
½ cup granulated sugar
½ cup brown sugar, packed
½ teaspoon baking soda
½ teaspoon salt
½ teaspoon cinnamon
1½ cups finely chopped
     apples, peeled

**CINNAMON BROWN SUGAR
GLAZE:**

½ cup brown sugar, packed
¼ cup unsalted butter
½ teaspoon cinnamon
½ teaspoon vanilla extract
1 tablespoon heavy cream

Preparation:

FOR THE CAKE:

- Preheat oven to 350°F.
- Grease an 8 × 8-inch baking pan and set aside.
- In a large bowl, mix the eggs with a hand mixer until foamy and light in color. Add the oil and vanilla and beat well.
- Stir in the flour, sugars, baking soda, salt, and cinnamon. Stir just until the flour has been incorporated, then add the chopped apples and stir into the batter.
- Scrape the thick batter into the prepared pan spreading the batter into the corners.
- Bake for 40 to 45 minutes, or until a toothpick inserted in the center comes out clean.
- Place the hot cake on a wire cake. While the cake is still hot, prepare the glaze.

FOR THE GLAZE:

- Combine all the ingredients into a saucepan. Cook over medium heat, stirring often, until the mixture comes to a gentle boil. Cook for 3 to 5 minutes.
- Spoon the hot glaze over the hot cake.
- Allow the glazed cake to cool completely before serving directly from the dish.

Baker's note

I used organic Fuji apples in this cake because that's what I like to snack on, but Red or Golden Delicious, Granny Smith or Gala apples would also work well in this recipe.

CHOCOLATE GINGERBREAD

Gingerbread has never been my favorite holiday treat, but adding chocolate to the batter has changed the way I think about gingerbread. The combination of cocoa and warm spices is really quite nice.

You need:

¼ cup unsweetened cocoa powder
¾ cup all-purpose flour
1 teaspoon ground cinnamon
1 teaspoon ground ginger
¼ teaspoon ground allspice
¼ teaspoon ground nutmeg
½ teaspoon baking soda
¼ teaspoon salt
¼ cup unsalted butter, melted
½ cup brown sugar, packed
¼ cup unsulfured molasses
1 large egg
¼ cup sour cream
½ teaspoon vanilla extract
½ cup semisweet chocolate chips

Preparation:

- Preheat oven to 350°F.
- Butter an 8-inch square baking dish and set aside.
- In a medium bowl, whisk together cocoa, flour, cinnamon, ginger, allspice, nutmeg baking soda, and salt. Set aside.
- In a large bowl, whisk together butter, brown sugar, molasses, egg, sour cream, and vanilla until smooth.
- Add flour mixture and stir just until moistened, being careful not to overmix. Stir in chocolate chips.
- Scrape batter into prepared pan and smooth top.
- Bake for 28 to 32 minutes or until a toothpick inserted in the center comes out clean.
- Transfer pan to a wire rack and let cool completely. Serve directly from dish.

PUMPKIN BUNDT CAKE WITH BROWN BUTTER GLAZE

I only have one recipe for pumpkin cake, and this is it. Pumpkin and brown butter are a match made in heaven. This cake is so moist, it just melts in your mouth.

You need:

PUMPKIN CAKE:
2 cups granulated sugar
4 large eggs
1 cup canola oil
1 teaspoon vanilla extract
2 cups all-purpose flour
2 teaspoon baking soda
2 teaspoon cinnamon
½ teaspoon salt
one 15-ounce can pure
   pumpkin

BROWN BUTTER GLAZE:
¼ cup unsalted butter
1¼ cups powdered sugar
2 tablespoons milk
½ teaspoon vanilla extract

Preparation:

FOR THE CAKE:
- Preheat oven to 350°F.
- Grease and flour a 9-inch Bundt pan and set aside.
- In a large bowl, beat sugar and eggs until well blended and light in color. Add oil and vanilla and continue to beat.
- Add the flour, baking soda, cinnamon, and salt to the egg mixture and stir to combine.
- Add pumpkin puree and mix well. Pour into prepared pan.
- Bake for 50 to 55 minutes or until a toothpick inserted into the center of the cake comes out clean.
- Let stand in pan for 10 minutes, then turn out onto baking rack to cool completely.
- Once the cake has cooled, place it on a serving platter and make the glaze.

FOR THE GLAZE:
- In a medium bowl add the powdered sugar and set aside while you make the brown butter.
- In a small saucepan, melt the butter over medium heat. Continue to cook, swirling the pot occasionally until the butter boils and becomes foamy. It will turn golden brown and start to smell nutty. Once the butter stops sizzling and the foam subsides, it is ready. Keep an eye on it because you don't want it to burn. This could take 5 to 8 minutes.
- Once the butter has browned, remove from the heat and pour the butter and the browned bits over the sugar. Add the milk and vanilla to the butter and sugar and whisk until smooth.
- Spoon the warm glaze over the cooled cake and allow the glaze to set before serving.
- Store at room temperature.

Chapter 2

CUPCAKES

BERRY LEMON CUPCAKES

These cupcakes are vibrant and taste like summer, but because this recipe uses frozen berries, you can make them any time of year. My mother-in-law declares these are the best cupcakes I've ever made, and I am not one to argue with her.

You need:

BERRY PUREE:
12 ounces frozen mixed berries
2 tablespoons granulated sugar

LEMON CUPCAKES:
2 cups all-purpose flour
1⅓ cups granulated sugar
1 teaspoon baking soda
½ teaspoon baking powder
½ teaspoon salt
⅓ cup canola oil
2 large eggs
¾ cup buttermilk
1 teaspoon vanilla extract
⅓ cup fresh lemon juice
1 tablespoon finely grated lemon zest

BERRY BUTTERCREAM:
⅓ cup reduced and chilled berry puree
1 cup unsalted butter, room temperature
3 cups powdered sugar, sifted
2 teaspoons fresh lemon juice

Baker's note
These cupcakes are simple to make but the berry puree needs to be prepared ahead of time and chilled before use. Plan ahead!

Preparation:

FOR THE BERRY PUREE:
- Place the frozen berries and sugar in a saucepan and cook over medium heat, stirring occasionally.
- The mixture will become very liquid and the fruit will soften. Cook over medium-low heat until the berries cook down to a pulp and the mixture thickens. Continue to cook, stirring frequently until the berry mixture has reduced by half. This could take up to 30 minutes.
- Place a metal sieve over a small mixing bowl. Pour the cooked and reduced fruit into the strainer and push the berries through. Discard the seeds.
- Pour berry puree into a measuring cup. You should have close to one-third cup puree. If you have much more than that, return the puree back to the saucepan and continue to cook down for a few more minutes, over medium heat. Cooking down the berries will result in a concentrated berry flavor without all the added water.
- Once you have one-third cup of berry puree, place in small bowl, cover and place in the refrigerator until well chilled.

FOR THE CUPCAKES:
- Preheat oven to 350°F.
- Line standard muffin tins with 24 paper liners. Set aside.
- In a large bowl, combine flour, sugar, baking soda, baking powder, and salt. Whisk to combine then add the oil, eggs, buttermilk, vanilla, and lemon juice. Stir in the lemon zest.
- Divide batter evenly between the lined cups.
- Bake for 18 to 20 minutes or until a toothpick inserted in the center comes out clean.
- Cool in pan for 5 minutes before carefully removing the cupcakes to a rack. Cool completely before frosting with berry buttercream.

FOR THE BUTTERCREAM:
- In a large bowl, cream butter with an electric mixer over medium-high speed until light and creamy.
- Add the chilled berry puree and beat the mixture until combined.
- Gradually add the powdered sugar to the butter mixture and beat until combined, scraping down the sides of the bowl as necessary. Pour in the fresh lemon juice and beat once more until incorporated.
- Pipe or mound frosting over cooled cupcakes.

Makes 24 cupcakes.

OREO CHEESECAKE CUPCAKES

You need:

CHEESECAKE FILLING:

8 ounces cream cheese, room
temperature
1 cup powdered sugar
½ teaspoon vanilla extract

CHOCOLATE CUPCAKES:

24 Oreos
1½ cups all-purpose flour
1¼ cups granulated sugar
¼ cup unsweetened cocoa
powder
1 teaspoon baking soda
½ teaspoon baking powder
½ teaspoon salt
⅓ cup canola oil
1 cup prepared coffee, room
temperature
1 teaspoon vanilla extract
2 large eggs, lightly beaten

OREO BUTTERCREAM:

½ cup unsalted butter, room
temperature
½ cup shortening, room
temperature
1 teaspoon vanilla extract
2 tablespoons milk
3-4 cups powdered sugar
14 Oreos, finely crushed in
food processor

GARNISH:

24 Oreos

Baker's note
The cream cheese mixture needs
to be made ahead of time and
chilled prior to making these
cupcakes. This step can be
made up to 3 days in advance.

Preparation:

FOR THE FILLING:

- Combine the cream cheese, vanilla, and powdered sugar in a medium bowl and mix well until blended and smooth.
- Transfer the mixture onto a piece of plastic wrap and shape into a log about 1½ inches in diameter.
- Smooth the plastic wrap tightly around the log, and reinforce with a piece of foil. Transfer to the freezer and chill until slightly firm, at least 2 to 3 hours.
- Once cream cheese log is sufficiently chilled, unwrap it and slice log into 24 equal pieces. If it's still too soft, you can scoop it instead. You need about 1 to 2 teaspoons of cream cheese mixture per cupcake. Keep it chilled until you're ready for it.

FOR THE CUPCAKES:

- Preheat oven to 350°F. Line cupcake tins with 24 paper liners. Place an Oreo in the bottom of each liner and set aside.
- In a large bowl, combine flour, sugar, cocoa powder, baking soda, baking powder, and salt. Using a wire whisk, blend the dry ingredients thoroughly.
- Add the oil, cooled coffee, vanilla, and eggs to the dry ingredients. Whisk until well incorporated and no lumps remain.
- Place one tablespoon of cupcake batter over the Oreos. Place cream cheese on top of that, then evenly divide the rest of the batter over the cream cheese between the 24 muffin tins.
- Bake the cupcakes for 18 to 20 minutes or until a toothpick inserted into the cake (not the cream cheese center) comes out clean. Allow to cool for 10 minutes, then place them on a rack to cool completely.

FOR THE BUTTERCREAM:

- In a large bowl, cream the butter, shortening, vanilla, and milk together until light and fluffy.
- Slowly add the powdered sugar, one cup at a time until desired sweetness is achieved, anywhere between 3 and 4 cups.
- Mix in crushed Oreos until well combined.
- If your frosting is too thick, add an additional tablespoon of milk to thin. If it's too thin, add more sugar until it's the texture you want.
- Pipe or mound frosting over cooled cupcakes. Top with more Oreos for garnish.
- Enjoy at room temperature.

Makes 24 cupcakes.

CARROT CUPCAKES WITH BROWN SUGAR CREAM CHEESE FROSTING

I am a carrot cake purist and don't like fruit or nuts in my cake. These cupcakes celebrate carrots and spice and all things nice.

You need:

CARROT CUPCAKES:
1¼ cups canola oil
1 cup granulated sugar
1 cup brown sugar, packed
1 teaspoon vanilla extract
4 large eggs
2 cups all-purpose flour
2 teaspoons baking powder
2 teaspoons baking soda
½ teaspoon salt
2 teaspoons ground cinnamon
3 cups coarsely grated carrots, packed

BROWN SUGAR CREAM CHEESE FROSTING:
12 ounces cream cheese, room temperature
½ cup unsalted butter, room temperature
1 cup brown sugar, packed
1 teaspoon ground cinnamon
½ teaspoon freshly grated nutmeg

Preparation:

FOR THE CUPCAKES:
- Preheat oven to 350°F.
- Line standard muffin tins with 24 paper liners. Set aside.
- In a large bowl, combine oil, sugars, and vanilla. Whisk to combine.
- Add the eggs, one at a time, beating well after each addition.
- Whisk in the flour, baking powder, baking soda, salt, and cinnamon.
- Stir in the grated carrots until well blended.
- Divide batter evenly between the lined cups.
- Bake for 20 to 22 minutes or until a toothpick inserted in the center comes out clean.
- Cool in pan for 5 minutes before carefully removing the cupcakes to a rack. Cool completely before frosting.

FOR THE FROSTING:
- In a large bowl, beat cream cheese and butter with an electric mixer over medium-high speed until creamy and smooth.
- Add the brown sugar and spices and beat on medium-high speed until fluffy. Use immediately.
- Pipe or mound frosting over cooled cupcakes.

Makes 24 cupcakes.

TEXAS SHEET CAKE CUPCAKES

My husband's favorite cake is Texas sheet cake, which is typically a thin, large chocolate cake covered in icing and pecans. I took the components of that cake and turned it into cupcakes. You get all the flavors of a Texas sheet cake rolled into a personal-sized dessert, topped with a hefty amount of fudgy pecan icing.

You need:

CHOCOLATE CUPCAKES:
1½ cups all-purpose flour
1¼ cups granulated sugar
¼ cup unsweetened cocoa powder
1 teaspoon baking soda
½ teaspoon baking powder
½ teaspoon salt
⅓ cup canola oil
1 cup water
1 teaspoon vanilla extract
2 eggs, lightly beaten

TOASTED PECAN FUDGE ICING:
½ cup pecans
3 tablespoons unsalted butter
2 tablespoons milk
4 teaspoons unsweetened cocoa powder
¼ teaspoon ground cinnamon
1⅓ cups powdered sugar, sifted
½ teaspoon vanilla extract

Preparation:

FOR THE CUPCAKES:
- Preheat oven to 350°F.
- Line standard muffin tins with 20 paper liners and set aside.
- In a large bowl, combine flour, sugar, cocoa powder, baking soda, baking powder, and salt. Using a wire whisk, blend the dry ingredients thoroughly.
- Add the oil, water, vanilla, and eggs to the dry ingredients. Whisk until well incorporated and no lumps remain.
- Evenly divide the batter between the paper liners.
- Bake for 18 to 20 minutes, or until a toothpick inserted into the center comes out clean.
- Allow to cool for 5 minutes in the pan, then place them on a rack to cool completely before topping with pecan fudge icing.

FOR THE ICING:
- While the oven is still on, place your pecans on a rimmed baking sheet and place in the oven for 10 minutes until the pecans become aromatic and have turned a slight golden brown, being careful not to burn them.
- Remove from the oven and allow them to cool on the baking sheet. Once cool, chop the pecans and set them aside.
- In a medium sauce pot, combine butter, milk, cocoa, and cinnamon. Stir over low heat until butter is melted.
- Add powdered sugar ⅓ cup at a time while continuing to stir until smooth. Stir in vanilla extract and chopped pecans.
- Take the pan off the heat but leave the icing in the pot. Allow the icing to cool for 15 to 30 minutes or until the pot is cool enough to touch. The icing will thicken as it cools. You want the icing to be thick enough to stay on top of the cupcake but not too thick that it doesn't spread. If your icing becomes hard and too thick to handle, place it back on the stove over low heat and stir until the desired consistency is met.
- Using a small ice cream scoop, place a small mound on top of each cupcake. The icing will spread slightly and possibly drip down the sides a bit, depending how warm your icing is. Divide evenly over each cupcake. Allow the icing to cool completely and set before enjoying.
- Store cupcakes at room temperature.
Makes 20 cupcakes.

PECAN PIE MINI CUPCAKES

Buttery, nutty, and gooey pecan pie flavor all in one bite!

You need:

½ cup all-purpose flour
1 cup brown sugar, packed
¼ teaspoon salt
½ teaspoon vanilla extract
⅔ cup unsalted butter, melted
2 large eggs
1 cup finely chopped pecans

Preparation:

- Preheat oven to 350°F.
- In a medium bowl, combine flour, sugar, salt, vanilla, melted butter, and eggs. Whisk to combine then stir in the chopped pecans. Mix well.
- Generously spray a miniature muffin tin with nonstick baking spray with flour. Fill each indention three-fourths of the way full.
- Bake in preheated oven for approximately 17 to 19 minutes.
- Cool for 2 minutes in the pan, then invert them onto a rack to cool completely.
- Store at room temperature.

Makes 24-30 mini cupcakes.

Baker's note
You need to unmold these from the pan pretty quickly after baking them, or they'll stick to the pan. Use a butter knife to gently loosen them if you have a few stubborn ones.

FERRERO ROCHER CUPCAKES

Chocolate hazelnut spread becomes the filling and topping for this dense, fudgy cupcake.

You need:

CUPCAKES:

½ cup unsalted butter, room temperature
½ cup granulated sugar
½ cup brown sugar, packed
4 large eggs
1 cup chocolate syrup
1 tablespoon vanilla extract
1 cup all-purpose flour

FILLING AND GARNISH:

one 13-ounce jar Nutella
16 Ferrero Rocher candies, unwrapped

Preparation:

FOR THE CUPCAKES:

- Preheat the oven to 325°F.
- Line a standard muffin tin with 16 paper or foil liners and set aside.
- In a large bowl, combine the butter and sugars. Using a hand mixer beat on medium speed until light and fluffy.
- Add the eggs one at a time beating well after each addition. Mix in the chocolate syrup and vanilla. Then add the flour and mix until just combined, being careful not to overbeat.
- Divide the batter evenly between the lined muffin cups, filling each cup no more than three-fourths full.
- Bake for 30 minutes, or until just set in the middle.
- Let the cupcakes cool in the pan for 10 minutes before removing to a rack to cool completely.

ASSEMBLY:

- Once cupcakes are completely cool, cut out a small piece, about an inch wide, from the top of the cupcake using a paring knife. Discard or eat the small pieces of cake that are removed from the cupcakes. This will create a well for the Nutella filling.
- Fill each cupcake with about 1 tablespoon of Nutella. Repeat until the Nutella has been evenly divided amongst the cupcakes. Top off each cupcake with a Ferrero Rocher candy, slighting pressing into the Nutella so it stays put.
- Store at room temperature in an airtight container.

Makes 16 cupcakes.

PIÑA COLADA MINI CHEESECAKES

You need:

CRUST:
3/4 cup graham cracker
   crumbs
2 tablespoons brown sugar,
   packed
2 tablespoons unsalted
   butter, melted

CHEESECAKE:
16 ounces cream cheese,
   room temperature
1/3 cup granulated sugar
2 large eggs
2/3 cup cream of coconut
8 ounces crushed pineapple,
   drained
1/2 teaspoon coconut extract
1/2 teaspoon rum extract

COCONUT WHIPPED CREAM:
1/2 cup heavy cream
3 tablespoons cream of
   coconut
1/2 teaspoon coconut extract
2 tablespoons powdered
   sugar

Preparation:

TO MAKE THE CRUST:
- Preheat oven to 325°F. Line standard muffin tins with 16 paper liners. Set aside.
- In a small bowl, combine the graham cracker crumbs and sugar. Mix to combine, then stir in the melted butter until the crumbs are evenly moistened.
- Evenly divide the moistened crumbs between the paper cups using about one heaping tablespoon per liner. Using your fingers or the bottom of a small juice glass, press the crumbs firmly into the bottom of the cupcake liners.
- Bake for 5 minutes, then cool.

TO MAKE THE CHEESECAKE:
- In a large bowl, beat the cream cheese with an electric mixer on medium speed until creamy and no lumps remain. Slowly add the sugar and mix until combined, scraping down the sides of the bowl as necessary.
- Add the eggs, one at a time, and beat until just combined. Scrape down the sides of the bowl. Add the cream of coconut, crushed pineapple, coconut, and rum extracts. Beat until well mixed and scrape down the bowl once more, but try and avoid overmixing the batter.
- Evenly divide the batter between the lined cups. They will be pretty full. This is okay.
- Bake for 18 to 20 minutes. They will puff slightly in the oven, and the center may be a little jiggly. As they cool, they will firm up.
- Cool to room temperature, then place the cheesecakes, still in the pans, in the refrigerator to chill for at least 2 hours.

TO MAKE THE COCONUT WHIPPED CREAM:
- In a medium bowl, combine the heavy cream, cream of coconut, coconut extract, and the powdered sugar. Using an electric mixer on medium speed beat the ingredients together until the mixture has doubled in volume and soft peaks form.
- Dollop the coconut cream over the tops of the cheesecakes before serving. Garnish with shredded coconut, pineapple chunks, or maraschino cherries, if desired.
- Store in an airtight container in the refrigerator for 3 to 5 days.

Baker's note
Cream of coconut is a sweetened liquid often sold in the grocery aisle where alcohol and drink mixes are sold. It is thicker and has a more concentrated flavor than coconut milk or water.

Chapter 3

COOKIES

PERFECT CHOCOLATE CHIP COOKIES

The perfect chocolate chip cookie for me is big and buttery, crisp on the edges and slightly chewy in the center. It's also important that they look as good as they taste, so there are plenty of chocolate chips in the cookie as well as on the top.

You need:

2¼ cups all-purpose flour
1 teaspoon baking soda
1 teaspoon salt
1 cup unsalted butter, room
    temperature
¾ cup granulated sugar
¾ cup brown sugar, packed
2 large eggs
1½ teaspoons vanilla extract
3 cups semisweet
    chocolate chips

Preparation:

- Preheat oven to 375°F.
- In a medium bowl, combine the flour, baking soda, and salt. Whisk to combine and set aside.
- In a large bowl, cream the butter and sugars together until light and fluffy, about 3 minutes.
- Add the eggs, one at a time, mixing well after each addition. Add the vanilla and mix well.
- Gradually add the flour mixture to the butter mixture and beat just until the flour has been mixed in. Stir 2 cups of the chocolate chips into the batter, reserving the remaining cup of chocolate chips for the tops of the cookies.
- Using a medium cookie scoop (1½ tablespoons), portion out the dough and top each mound of dough with 3 to 4 chocolate chips.
- Place the cookie dough 3 inches apart onto ungreased cookie sheets.
- Bake for 10 to 13 minutes or until lightly golden.
- Allow cookies to cool on pan for about 5 minutes before removing to a rack to cool completely.

Make 3 dozen 4-inch cookies.

Baker's note
If you want smaller cookies, you can use a small cookie scoop (2 teaspoons) to portion out the dough. Bake for 8 to 10 minutes. Makes about 6 to 7 dozen.

AUNT MARY'S SUGAR COOKIES

My great aunt Mary has been making a version of these tender cookies for as long as I can remember. These aren't the types of cookies that need icing. Instead they're simply decorated with sprinkles and colored sugar before baking.

You need:

1 cup unsalted butter, softened
1½ cups powdered sugar
1 large egg
1 teaspoon vanilla extract
½ teaspoon almond extract
2½ cups all-purpose flour
2 teaspoons baking powder
Sprinkles and colored sugar for decorating

Preparation:

- Cream butter and powdered sugar together in a large bowl.
- Stir in egg, vanilla, and almond extract until well combined. Stir in flour and baking powder.
- Divide dough in half and form them into disks. Wrap well with plastic wrap and refrigerate discs for at least 3 hours or overnight.
- Preheat oven to 375°F.
- Roll out dough onto a lightly floured surface and cut out shapes using your favorite cookie cutters.
- Decorate the cookies by sprinkling them with colored sugar and sprinkles. Put cookies back into the fridge for 20 to 30 minutes until they are firm to the touch. This will help keep the cookies from spreading while they bake.
- Bake for 8 to 12 minutes or until the edges turn a light golden brown. This will vary depending on the size of your cookies.
- Allow cookies to cool on the pan for 5 minutes before removing them to a rack to cool completely.

Makes about 4 dozen cookies.

Baker's note
Part of the fun of baking sugar cookies is using different shapes and sizes of cutters. Be sure when baking that you put the smaller cookies on one sheet and the larger cookies on another, as they will have different baking times.
Once well wrapped, the cookie dough will keep in the freezer for up to 3 months. You can also freeze the baked and cooled cookies for just as long.

PECAN BUTTER BALLS

My neighbors introduced me to this wonderful cookie years ago. At Christmastime, when they bring over a tin of homemade cookies, these are the ones I reach for first.

You need:

1 cup unsalted butter, room
   temperature
¼ cup granulated sugar
½ teaspoon salt
2 teaspoons vanilla extract
2 cups all-purpose flour
1½ cups finely chopped
   pecans
1 to 2 cups powdered sugar
   for coating

Preparation:

- Preheat oven to 350°F.
- In a large bowl, cream butter and sugar together. Add salt and vanilla and mix well.
- Slowly add the flour to the butter mixture just until it forms a dough.
- Add the chopped nuts and mix until just combined.
- Using a small cookie scoop (2 teaspoons), portion out the dough into balls and place on parchment lined cookie sheets about an inch apart.
- Bake 28 to 30 minutes or until lightly golden.
- As soon as they come out of the oven, roll them in powdered sugar while the cookies are still hot. Be careful because the cookies are extremely hot and fragile. Place cookies on a cooling rack.
- Once cookies have cooled completely, roll them in powdered sugar again.

Makes 60–70 cookies.

Baker's note
You can also place the powdered sugar in a gallon-sized, heavy-duty zip-top bag to coat the cookies with. Place 4 to 5 cookies in the bag at a time and give a gentle shake. Just be careful because the bag may get hot from the cookies.

MIDNIGHT CHOCOLATE CHIP COOKIES

You need:

1¾ cups all-purpose flour

½ cup unsweetened cocoa powder

1½ teaspoons espresso powder

½ teaspoon ground cinnamon

1 teaspoon baking soda

½ teaspoon salt

1 cup unsalted butter, room temperature

¾ cup granulated sugar

¾ cup brown sugar, packed

2 large eggs

1½ teaspoons vanilla extract

2 cups semisweet chocolate chips

Preparation:

- Preheat oven to 375°F.
- In a medium bowl, combine the flour, cocoa powder, espresso powder, cinnamon, baking soda, and salt. Whisk to combine and set aside.
- In a large bowl, cream the butter and sugars together until light and fluffy, about 3 minutes.
- Add the eggs, one at a time, mixing well after each addition. Add the vanilla and mix well.
- Gradually add the flour mixture to the butter mixture and beat just until the flour has been mixed in. Stir the chocolate chips into the batter.
- Using a medium cookie scoop (1½ tablespoons), portion out the dough.
- Place the cookie dough 3 inches apart on ungreased cookie sheets and bake for 10 to 11 minutes. Do not overbake.
- Allow cookies to cool on pan for about 5 minutes before removing to a rack to cool completely.

Make 3 dozen 4-inch cookies.

OATMEAL CREAM PIES

These are not actually pies, but two buttery and chewy oatmeal raisin cookies sandwiched together with honey sweetened mascarpone cream. I came up with this idea on a whim several years ago when I wanted to bake for a special family friend and have been making them ever since. I can't help but think of her every time I whip up a batch.

You need:

OATMEAL COOKIES:

1½ cups all-purpose flour
1 teaspoon baking soda
1 teaspoon ground cinnamon
½ teaspoon salt
1 cup unsalted butter, room
    temperature
1 cup brown sugar, packed
½ cup granulated sugar
2 large eggs
1 teaspoon vanilla extract
3 cups old-fashioned oats
1 cup raisins

MASCARPONE CREAM FILLING:

8 ounces mascarpone cheese,
    room temperature
4 ounces cream cheese, room
    temperature
3 to 4 tablespoons honey
½ cup powdered sugar, sifted

Preparation:

FOR THE COOKIES:

- Preheat oven to 350°F.
- In a medium bowl, combine the flour, baking soda, cinnamon, and salt. Whisk to combine and set aside.
- In a large bowl, cream together the butter and sugars until creamy. Add eggs and vanilla. Mix well.
- Add the flour mixture to the creamed butter and mix until fully incorporated. Stir in the oats and raisins.
- Using a medium cookie scoop (1½ tablespoons), portion out the dough and place on ungreased cookie sheets about 3 inches apart.
- Bake for 12 to 15 minutes or until golden brown.
- Cool 5 minutes on the cookie sheet, then remove to a rack to cool completely. While the cookies are cooling, make the filling.

FOR THE FILLING:

- In a medium bowl, combine the cheeses and mix with an electric mixer until creamy and lump free. Mix in desired amount of honey. Then mix in the sugar and beat until well incorporated.

TO ASSEMBLE THE CREAM PIES:

- Place about 1 to 2 tablespoons of filling on the underside of one cookie and top with an additional cookie. Gently squeeze together to allow the filling to come to the edges.
- Refrigerate overnight to allow the cookies to soften and the flavors to melt together.

Makes about 18 to 20 oatmeal cookie sandwiches.

Baker's note
These cookie sandwiches get better by the day. Wrap and refrigerate them and enjoy them for up to a week.

CINNAMON PEANUT BUTTER COOKIES

I discovered a new peanut butter that was mixed with cinnamon and raisins. My son and I could not get enough of the pairing, and it later became an inspiration for these cookies.

You need:

CINNAMON SUGAR:
⅓ cup granulated sugar
½ teaspoon ground
   cinnamon

PEANUT BUTTER COOKIES:
1½ cups all-purpose flour
1½ teaspoons ground
   cinnamon
½ teaspoon baking soda
½ teaspoon salt
½ cup unsalted butter, room
   temperature
½ cup creamy peanut butter
1 cup brown sugar, packed
1 large egg
½ teaspoon vanilla extract

Preparation:

FOR THE CINNAMON SUGAR:
- In a small bowl, combine the ⅓ cup of sugar and the ½ teaspoon cinnamon. Mix to combine and set aside.

FOR THE COOKIES:
- Preheat oven to 350°F.
- In a medium bowl, combine the flour, cinnamon, baking soda, and salt. Whisk to combine and set aside.
- In a large bowl, cream the butter, peanut butter, and sugar using an electric mixer on medium speed until light and creamy. Stir in the egg and vanilla and mix to combine.
- Slowly add the dry mixture to the creamed mixture and mix until all the flour is incorporated, scraping down the sides of the bowl as needed.
- Using a small cookie scoop (2 teaspoons), portion out the dough. Roll the dough in between your hands to form balls. Roll the cookie dough into the cinnamon sugar mixture, coating them completely.
- Place on an ungreased cookie sheet, 2 inches apart. Flatten the dough very slightly to keep the balls from rolling around.
- Bake for 9 to 10 minutes or until lightly golden.
- Allow cookies to cool on pan for 5 minutes before removing to a rack to cool completely.

Makes about 4 dozen cookies.

COWBOY COOKIES

There is something for everyone in this cookie.

You need:

1 cup all-purpose flour
1 teaspoon baking powder
1 teaspoon baking soda
1 teaspoon ground cinnamon
½ teaspoon salt
½ cup unsalted butter, room temperature
½ cup brown sugar, packed
½ cup granulated sugar
1 large egg
1 teaspoon vanilla extract
1 cup old-fashioned oats
½ cup shredded coconut
¾ cup chopped pecans
1 cup semisweet chocolate chips
⅔ cup pretzels, broken into small pieces

Preparation:

- Preheat oven to 350°F.
- In a medium bowl, combine flour, baking powder, baking soda, cinnamon, and salt. Whisk to combine and set aside.
- In a large bowl, beat butter, and sugars on medium speed with an electric mixer until light and creamy.
- Add egg and vanilla. Mix until combined.
- Stir the flour mixture into the butter and mix until just combined.
- Add the oats, coconut, pecans, chocolate chips, and pretzel pieces. Mix dough until fully incorporated.
- Using a medium ice cream scoop (1½ tablespoons), portion out the dough onto an ungreased baking sheet, 3 inches apart. Flatten the cookie dough slightly before baking.
- Bake for about 13 to 15 minutes, until edges are lightly browned.
- Allow cookies to cool on pan for 5 minutes before removing to a rack to cool completely.

Makes about 2½ dozen cookies.

BROWN SUGAR SHORTBREAD

I created these shortbread cookies for my son, Hayden. I can't help but think of him clapping and smiling while I roll out dough and sing,

> "Pat-a-cake, pat-a-cake, baker's man,
> Bake me a cake as fast as you can;
> Pat it, prick it, and mark it with 'H,'
> Put it in the oven for 'Hayden' and me."

You need:

1 cup unsalted butter, room temperature
⅔ cup brown sugar, packed
2 cups all-purpose flour
¼ cup cornstarch
⅛ teaspoon salt

Preparation:

- Preheat oven to 350°F.
- In a large bowl, combine butter and sugar. Cream together until light and fluffy.
- Add the flour, cornstarch, and salt and mix until combined.
- Place the dough between two large pieces of parchment paper and flatten slightly. Using a rolling pin, roll the dough into a rectangle about 12 × 6-inches wide and 3/8-inch thick.
- Slide the dough and parchment paper onto a cookie sheet, and place in the refrigerator to chill for a minimum of 30 minutes.
- Once dough is sufficiently chilled, cut into rectangles, about 2½ × 1-inch wide.
- Place the shortbread fingers on ungreased cookie sheets, placing them about 2 inches apart.
- Gently prick the dough evenly with a fork. If the dough has softened, put it back into the refrigerator to chill until the dough has firmed back up.
- Bake the shortbread for 12 to 15 minutes, or until very lightly golden.
- Allow the shortbread to cool for 5 minutes on the pan before removing to a rack to cool completely.

Makes about 30 shortbread cookies.

FRUIT PIZZA

I learned to make this dessert when I was in high school. Back then, I used refrigerated sugar cookie dough. This recipe is just as simple to make but so much fresher and can be topped with any kind of fruit you like.

You need:

CRUST:
½ cup unsalted butter, melted
1 cup granulated sugar
1 large egg
1 teaspoon vanilla extract
1½ cups all-purpose flour
½ teaspoon baking soda
½ teaspoon salt

FILLING:
8 ounces cream cheese, room temperature
½ cup lemon curd

TOPPING:
3-4 cups fresh fruit

Preparation:

FOR THE CRUST:
- Preheat oven to 350°F.
- In a large bowl, mix melted butter and sugar together. Add the egg and stir in the vanilla until thoroughly combined.
- Add the flour, baking soda, and salt to the butter mixture and stir until a dough forms and the flour is fully incorporated.
- Scrape ball of dough out onto a large piece of parchment. With your hands, form dough into a 9-inch circle about 1-inch thick.
- Place the parchment paper onto a round pizza pan or large-rimmed baking sheet.
- Bake for 16 to 18 minutes until golden brown and the center has puffed up slightly.
- Cool on pan for 5 minutes before removing the cookie and the parchment paper to a cooling rack.

FOR THE FILLING:
- In a medium bowl, beat cream cheese with an electric mixer until light and creamy. Add the lemon curd and beat until just combined, scraping down the sides of the bowl as necessary.
- Scrape the cream cheese filling onto the center of the cooled cookie, and spread it out to the edges.
- Top the cookie with berries and slices of fresh fruit.
- Store leftovers in the refrigerator, well wrapped.

Makes one 11 x 12-inch fruit pizza

Baker's note
Fresh berries, peeled and sliced kiwi, peaches, and canned mandarin oranges that have been drained work well. Avoid watery fruits such as pineapple and melons and fruits that oxidize such as apples, bananas, and pears.

GLAZED LEMON COOKIES

A four-and-a-half-year-old little girl named Lily dreamt up these cookies. She got the brilliant idea of lemon cookies stuck in her head, so I went to the kitchen and created this recipe in her honor. They are bright and lemony and use both lemon juice and zest in the cookie and the glaze.

You need:

LEMON COOKIES:

½ cup unsalted butter, melted
1 cup granulated sugar
1 large egg
1 tablespoon finely grated
    lemon zest
1 teaspoon fresh lemon juice
½ teaspoon vanilla extract
1¾ cups all-purpose flour
½ teaspoon baking soda
¼ teaspoon salt

LEMON GLAZE:

¾ cup powdered sugar
1 teaspoon finely grated
    lemon zest
2 tablespoons fresh lemon
    juice

Preparation:

TO MAKE THE COOKIES:

- Preheat oven to 350°F.
- In a large bowl, mix melted butter and sugar together. Add the egg, lemon zest, lemon juice, and vanilla, and stir until thoroughly combined.
- Add the flour, baking soda, and salt to the butter mixture, and stir until a dough forms and the flour is fully incorporated.
- Using a small cookie scoop (2 teaspoons), portion out the dough. Roll the dough in between your hands to form balls.
- Place on an ungreased cookie sheet, 2 to 3 inches apart.
- Bake for 10 minutes or until lightly golden.
- Allow cookies to cool on pan for 5 minutes before removing to a rack to cool completely.

TO MAKE THE GLAZE:

- In a small bowl, whisk together the powdered sugar, lemon zest, and juice.
- Spoon about ½ teaspoon of glaze over each cookie. Allow the glaze to set before serving.

Makes about 3½ dozen cookies.

PEANUT BUTTER AND JAM THUMBPRINTS

My friend Heather makes the best peanut butter blossom cookies. She generously shared her recipe with me, and I adapted them to create these thumbprint cookies filled with jam. Perfect for an after school treat with a cold glass of milk.

You need:

½ cup granulated sugar

½ cup packed brown sugar

½ cup unsalted butter, softened

⅔ cup creamy peanut butter

3 tablespoons milk

1 teaspoon vanilla extract

1 large egg

1¾ cup all-purpose flour

1 teaspoon baking soda

¼ teaspoon salt

⅓ cup granulated sugar

⅔ to ¾ cup fruit jam, any flavor

Preparation:

- Preheat oven to 375°F.
- In a medium bowl, combine flour, baking soda, and salt. Whisk to combine and set aside.
- In a large bowl, cream together both sugars, butter, and peanut butter using an electric mixer, until light and fluffy. Gradually add the milk, vanilla, and egg, beating until well combined.
- Gradually add the flour mixture to the peanut butter mixture, beating on low speed until the flour is fully incorporated, scraping down the sides of the bowl as necessary.
- Place remaining ⅓ cup sugar in a small bowl. Using a small cookie scoop (2 teaspoons), portion the cookie dough into balls. Roll cookie dough balls in sugar coating them evenly.
- Place sugar-coated balls on an ungreased cookie sheet, 2 to 3 inches apart.
- Bake for 8 to 10 minutes or until lightly golden brown.
- Remove from the oven and using the handle of a wooden spoon, immediately press an indention into the center of the warm cookies.
- Place jam in a microwave safe bowl. Heat for 10 seconds and stir to loosen up the jam.
- Fill the centers with a ½ teaspoon of jam and allow the cookies to cool for 5 to 10 minutes before removing to a rack to cool completely.

Makes about 5 dozen cookies.

Baker's note
If your jam is thin enough to pour, there is no need to heat it. If you accidentally overheat it and it becomes runny, let it cool and thicken before using. Any fruit jam will work; use your favorite flavors. I used grape, peach, and plum jam.

GIANT CHOCOLATE CHIP COOKIE

This giant cookie comes together in less than 20 minutes and is perfect for feeding a crowd.

You need:

½ cup unsalted butter, melted
½ cup brown sugar, packed
½ cup granulated sugar
1 large egg
1 teaspoon vanilla extract
½ teaspoon baking soda
½ teaspoon salt
1½ cups all-purpose flour
½ cup rolled old-fashioned oats
½ cup semisweet chocolate chips
¼ cup M&M's

Preparation:

- Preheat oven to 350°F.
- In a large bowl, mix melted butter with both granulated and brown sugar. Add the egg and stir in the vanilla until thoroughly combined.
- Stir in the baking soda, salt, and flour.
- Add the oats and chocolate chips, and stir until just combined.
- Scrape ball of dough out onto a large piece of parchment. With your hands, form dough into a 9-inch circle about 1 inch thick. Smooth out the top and decorate with candy.
- Place the parchment paper onto a round pizza pan or large rimmed baking sheet.
- Bake for 16 to 18 minutes until golden brown and the center has puffed up slightly.
- Cool on pan for 5 minutes before removing the cookie and the parchment paper to a cooling rack.
- Store leftovers in an airtight container.

Makes one 11 x 12-inch cookie.

Baker's note
My brother made this cookie for his girlfriend and used the colored candy on top to spell out a message and make a heart. Use your imagination and have fun.

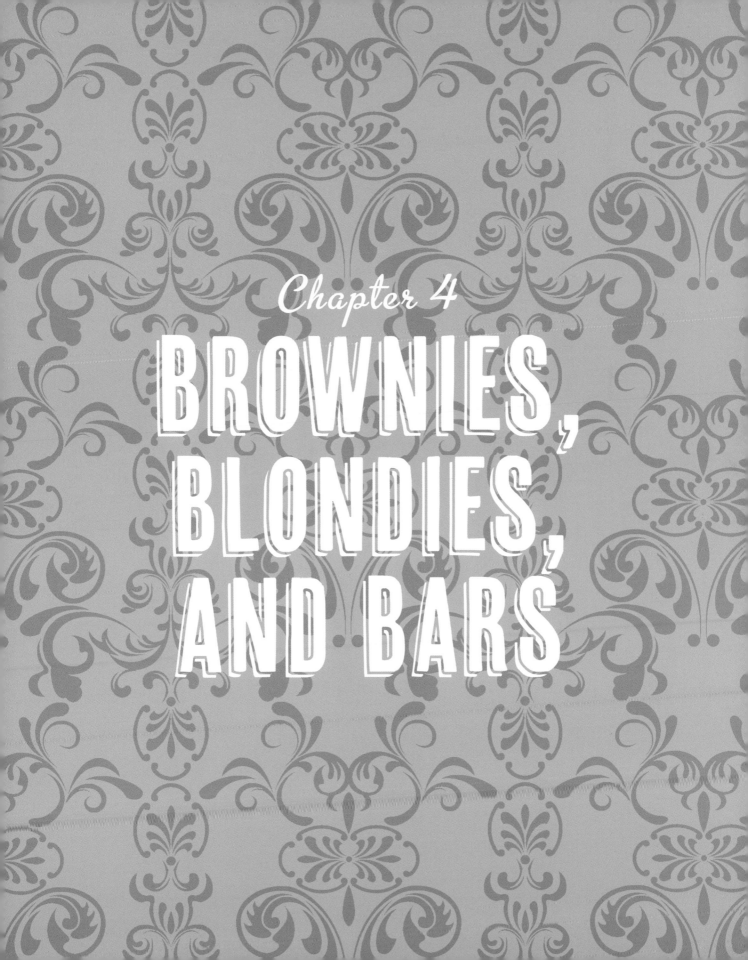

Chapter 4

BROWNIES, BLONDIES, AND BARS

BROWNED BUTTER TOFFEE ALMOND BLONDIES

You need:

½ cup unsalted butter
1 cup all-purpose flour
½ teaspoon baking powder
⅛ teaspoon salt
1 cup brown sugar, packed
1 large egg
1 teaspoon vanilla extract
½ teaspoon almond extract
⅓ cup sliced almonds (reserve a few for the top)
⅓ cup toffee bits

Preparation:

- Preheat oven to 350°F.
- Grease an 8-inch baking pan and line with parchment, allowing the ends of the paper to hang over two opposite edges of the pan.
- In a small saucepan, melt the butter over medium heat. Continue to cook, swirling the pot occasionally until the butter boils and becomes foamy. It will turn golden brown and start to smell nutty. Once the butter stops sizzling and the foam subsides, it is ready. Keep an eye on it because you don't want it to burn. This could take 5 to 8 minutes. Once it's browned, remove from the heat and allow it to cool slightly.
- In a medium bowl, whisk together the flour, baking powder, and salt. Set aside.
- Put the browned butter and the brown sugar in a large mixing bowl and stir until smooth.
- Add the eggs, vanilla, and almond extract, and mix until thoroughly combined.
- Stir in the flour mixture, followed by the almonds and toffee bits.
- Pour the batter into the prepared pan and smooth the top with an offset spatula. Press a few almonds on top for garnish, if desired.
- Bake for 23 to 25 minutes, until the top is golden brown.
- Remove the pan from the oven and let cool completely on a wire rack. Cut the blondies into bars.
- Store at room temperature.

Baker's note

The brown butter in this recipe really elevates the flavor in these blondies. But if you're pressed for time, you can substitute regular unsalted melted butter in its place.

ALMOND JOY BROWNIE BITES

I created this recipe with my mom in mind. She has mentioned a few times that she wishes the famous coconut almond candy was made with dark chocolate instead of milk chocolate, so I combined all three flavors in one delicious brownie bite.

You need:

COCONUT FILLING:
1 cup packed shredded coconut
¼ cup sweetened condensed milk
¼ teaspoon vanilla extract
¼ teaspoon almond extract

BROWNIES:
3 tablespoons unsalted butter, melted
1 tablespoon canola oil
1 large egg
½ teaspoon vanilla extract
⅔ cup granulated sugar
⅓ cup all-purpose flour
¼ cup unsweetened cocoa powder
¼ teaspoon baking powder
⅛ teaspoon salt

CHOCOLATE GANACHE:
¼ cup heavy cream
2 ounces semisweet chocolate, chopped
24 whole almonds

Baker's note

Don't get frightened by fancy words like ganache. It is just a mixture of warm cream and chocolate. Often used as a topping for for cakes, cupcakes, pies, and tarts.

Preparation:

FOR THE FILLING:
• In a small bowl, combine coconut, condensed milk, vanilla, and almond extract. Stir to combine and set aside.

FOR THE BROWNIES:
• Preheat oven to 350°F.
• Spray a mini muffin tin with nonstick baking spray and set aside.
• In a medium bowl, whisk together the butter, oil, egg, and vanilla. Add the sugar and whisk to combine.
• Add the flour, cocoa, baking powder, and salt to the sugar mixture. Whisk until the dry ingredients are fully incorporated and no lumps remain. Batter will be grainy.
• Divide the batter evenly between the prepared pan.
• Bake for 13 to 15 minutes or until a toothpick inserted comes out mostly clean.
• Using the handle of a wooden spoon, gently press down the center of the brownie, creating a cup to hold the filling.
• Allow the brownie cups to cool for 5 minutes before carefully removing them to a rack to cool completely.

FOR THE GANACHE:
• Place the chocolate in a small mixing bowl.
• In a small saucepan, heat heavy cream over medium heat but do not boil. Immediately pour the cream over the chocolate and let it rest for 5 minutes.
• Gently stir the chocolate until it's melted and the cream and chocolate are fully incorporated. Do not whisk the mixture or you'll incorporate air bubbles. Allow the chocolate mixture to rest for 10 to 15 minutes to cool and thicken.

ASSEMBLY:
• Evenly divide the coconut mixture between the cooled brownie cups.
• Top each with a whole almonds, then top with a spoonful of thickened chocolate ganache.
• Allow the ganache to set before serving.
• Store room temperature, covered.

Makes 24 mini brownie bites.

CHOCOLATE CRANBERRY OAT BARS

You need:

1½ cups all-purpose flour
1 teaspoon baking soda
1 teaspoon ground cinnamon
½ teaspoon salt
1 cup unsalted butter, room temperature
¾ cup brown sugar, packed
½ cup granulated sugar
2 large eggs
1 teaspoon vanilla extract
3 cups old-fashioned oats
1 cup chocolate covered cranberries
½ cup dried cranberries

Preparation:

- Preheat oven to 350°F.
- In a medium bowl, combine the flour, baking soda, cinnamon, and salt. Whisk to combine and set aside.
- In a large bowl, cream together the butter and sugars until creamy. Add eggs and vanilla. Mix well.
- Add the flour mixture to the creamed butter and mix until fully incorporated. Stir in the oats, chocolate covered cranberries, and the dried cranberries.
- Press dough into the bottom of an ungreased 9 × 13-inch baking pan.
- Bake for 30 to 35 minutes or until golden brown.
- Allow the pan to cool completely before serving.
- Cut into bars. Store at room temperature.

BLUEBERRY CITRUS BARS

Lemon or lime? When you just can't decide, turn to these zesty citrus bars loaded with fresh blueberries.

You need:

GRAHAM CRUST:

1¼ cups graham cracker crumbs

6 tablespoons butter, melted

¼ cup granulated sugar

CITRUS FILLING:

2 large egg yolks

one 14-ounce can sweetened condensed milk

¼ cup fresh lemon juice

¼ cup fresh lime juice

1 teaspoon finely grated lemon zest

1 teaspoon finely grated lime zest

1 cup fresh blueberries

Preparation:

FOR THE CRUST:

- Preheat oven to 350°F.
- Lightly butter an 8 × 8-inch baking dish and set aside.
- In a medium bowl, combine the graham cracker crumbs, melted butter, and sugar. Stir until graham cracker crumbs are moist and resemble sand.
- Press crumbs firmly into the bottom and slightly up the sides of buttered pan.
- Bake for 10 minutes.
- While the crust is cooling, prepare the filling.

TO MAKE THE FILLING:

- In a medium bowl, combine the egg yolks and condensed milk. Whisk together, then stir in the lemon and lime juice and zest. Gently whisk until fully incorporated.
- Using a rubber spatula, gently fold in the three-quarters of the blueberries, reserving the rest for the top.
- Pour the filling evenly over the graham cracker crust then top with the remaining blueberries.
- Bake for 15 minutes or until set.
- Cool for 10 minutes at room temperature, then refrigerate until completely chilled, at least 2 hours or overnight.
- Cut into bars and serve.

CHOCOLATE CHERRY BROWNIE KISSES

You need:

BROWNIES:

3 tablespoons unsalted butter, melted

1 tablespoon canola oil

1 large egg

½ teaspoon vanilla extract

⅔ cup granulated sugar

⅓ cup all-purpose flour

¼ cup unsweetened cocoa powder

¼ teaspoon baking powder

⅛ teaspoon salt

FILLING:

⅓ cup semisweet chocolate chips

one 10-ounce jar maraschino cherries, drained and patted dry (reserve the cherry liquid for use in the frosting)

CHERRY FROSTING:

¼ cup unsalted butter, room temperature

2 ounces cream cheese, room temperature

¾ cup powdered sugar, sifted

1 tablespoon maraschino cherry juice

½ teaspoon vanilla extract

Preparation:

FOR THE BROWNIES:

- Preheat oven to 350°F.
- Spray a mini muffin tin with nonstick baking spray and set aside.
- In a medium bowl, whisk together the butter, oil, egg, and vanilla. Add the sugar and whisk to combine.
- Add the flour, cocoa, baking powder, and salt to the sugar mixture. Whisk until the dry ingredients are fully incorporated and no lumps remain. Batter will be grainy.
- Divide the batter evenly between the prepared pan.
- Bake for 13 to 15 minutes or until a toothpick inserted comes out mostly clean.
- Using the handle of a wooden spoon, gently press down the center of the brownie, creating a cup to hold the filling.
- While the brownie cups are still hot, place 3 chocolate chips into the center. Let sit for a couple minutes to soften the chocolate then place a whole cherry into the brownie cups, gently pressing them into the chocolate.
- Allow the brownie cups to cool for 5 minutes before carefully removing them to a rack to cool completely. While they cool, make the frosting.

FOR THE FROSTING:

- In a medium bowl, combine the butter and cream cheese and beat until creamy.
- Add the powdered sugar and mix until fully incorporated, scraping down the sides of the bowl as necessary.
- Add the maraschino cherry juice and the vanilla and whisk to combine.
- Put the frosting in a piping bag and pipe over the cooled brownie bites, or simply dollop a spoonful of frosting onto each brownie
- Store at room temperature.

Makes 24 brownie bites.

SNICKERDOODLE CREAM CHEESE BLONDIES

This bar takes two of my favorite foods—snickerdoodles and cream cheese and combines them into one decadent bar with a creamy center and a crunchy, crackly top.

You need:

CREAM CHEESE FILLING:
8 ounces cream cheese, room temperature
¼ cup granulated sugar
1 large egg

BLONDIE BATTER:
1¼ cup all-purpose flour
¾ teaspoon ground cinnamon
¾ teaspoon baking powder
¼ teaspoon salt
½ cup unsalted butter, room temperature
1 cup brown sugar, packed
1 large egg
1 teaspoon vanilla extract
2 tablespoons milk

CINNAMON SUGAR TOPPING:
1½ tablespoons granulated sugar
½ teaspoon ground cinnamon

Preparation:

- Preheat oven to 350°F.
- Line an 8 × 8-inch baking dish with foil. Lightly spray with nonstick baking spray and set aside.

FOR THE FILLING:
- In medium bowl, beat cream cheese with an electric mixer until smooth. Add the sugar and egg and beat until combined, set aside.

FOR THE BLONDIES:
- In a small bowl, combine the flour, cinnamon, baking powder, and salt. Whisk together and set aside.
- In a large bowl, cream together the butter and sugar, using an electric mixer at medium speed until light and creamy. Add egg, vanilla, and milk and beat until combined.
- Using a rubber spatula, stir the flour mixture into the butter mixture and continue stirring until no traces of flour remain.
- Scrape half the batter into the bottom of the prepared pan and smooth it out to the corners.
- Pour the cream cheese mixture over the batter, then dollop the remaining batter over the cream cheese.
- Gently spread the batter trying to piece it together. If the cream cheese peeks through that's okay, just cover the top as much as you can.
- In a small bowl, mix cinnamon and sugar for the topping. Sprinkle the topping evenly over the batter.
- Bake for 45 to 55 minutes or until a toothpick inserted into the center comes out clean.
- Cool completely before serving.
- Serve chilled or at room temperature.

BROWN BUTTER AND SPICE RICE CRISPY TREATS

Browning the butter elevates these treats to a whole new level. These are not your ordinary marshmallow treats.

You need:

7 cups puffed rice cereal
½ cup unsalted butter
one 10-ounce bag (about 5 cups) mini marshmallows
1 teaspoon ground cinnamon
¼ teaspoon freshly ground nutmeg
⅛ teaspoon ground ginger

Preparation:

- Grease a 9 × 13-inch pan with softened butter and set aside.
- Measure out the cereal and place in a large bowl. Set aside.
- In a large saucepan, melt the butter over medium heat. Continue to cook, swirling the pot occasionally until the butter boils and becomes foamy. It will turn golden brown and start to smell nutty. Once the butter stops sizzling and the foam subsides, it is ready. Keep an eye on it because you don't want it to burn. This could take 5 to 8 minutes.
- Once the butter has browned, add the bag of marshmallows and stir. Continue stirring until the marshmallows have completely melted. Be careful because the mixture will be hot.
- Stir the cinnamon, nutmeg, and ginger into the marshmallow mixture and mix until combined.
- Quickly add the cereal to the marshmallow and spice mixture and stir until everything is well coated.
- Scrape the mixture into your buttered dish. With buttered hands, gently press the cereal evenly into the corners and smooth the top. The mixture will be hot. Be careful.
- Let cool completely and cut into bars.
- Store at room temperature.

ALMOND JAM BARS

These bars are so buttery, crunchy, and gooey. My favorite jam to use is Fredericksburg peach, but you can use whatever homemade or store bought jam you like.

You need:

1½ cups all-purpose flour
½ teaspoon ground cinnamon
¼ teaspoon salt
¼ teaspoon baking powder
½ cup unsalted butter, room temperature
½ cup brown sugar, packed
¼ cup granulated sugar
1 large egg yolk
¾ cup sliced almonds
⅔ cup fruit jam, any flavor

Preparation:

- Preheat oven to 350°F.
- Butter an 8 × 8-inch baking dish and set aside.
- In a small bowl, whisk together flour, cinnamon, salt, and baking powder.
- In a large bowl, cream butter and sugars together using an electric mixer on medium-high speed until light and fluffy. Beat in the egg yolk.
- Reduce speed to low and gradually add the dry ingredients to the butter mixture. Stir in the almonds.
- Gently press half of the almond mixture into the bottom and slightly up the sides of your prepared dish.
- Place the jam in a small bowl and whisk to loosen it up. Pour the jam onto the almond layer and spread evenly with the back of a spoon.
- Sprinkle the remaining almond mixture over the top all the way to the edges of the pan. Gently press together to form top layer, sealing in the jam.
- Bake for 30 to 35 minutes or until the top is golden brown and slightly puffed and cracked in the center.
- Cool the bars in the dish completely before serving.
- Store at room temperature.

LICK-THE-BOWL BROWNIES

Fudgy on the inside and chewy on the edges with a thin crackly top.

You need:

⅓ cup unsweetened cocoa powder
⅔ cup all-purpose flour
½ teaspoon salt
½ cup unsalted butter
2 tablespoons canola oil
4 ounces chopped semisweet chocolate or ¾ cup semisweet chocolate chips
1¼ cups granulated sugar
2 large eggs
2 teaspoons vanilla extract
1 teaspoon espresso powder

Preparation:

- Preheat oven to 350°F.
- Coat an 8 × 8-inch baking pan with softened butter. Line the pan with two pieces of parchment paper. Make sure the edges are long enough to drape over the sides of the pan for easy brownie removal. Set aside.
- In small bowl, whisk together cocoa, flour, and salt. Set aside.
- In a large microwave safe bowl, combine the butter and oil. Heat in the microwave until butter is melted, about 1 minute. Add the chocolate and stir gently until it melts. Microwave for an additional 30 seconds, if necessary. Continue to stir until the mixture is smooth.
- Add the sugar and whisk until fully incorporated. The mixture will be grainy. Allow to cool slightly.
- Add eggs, vanilla, and espresso powder to the cooled chocolate mixture and beat with an electric mixer on medium-high speed for a full 4 minutes. Since there are no chemical leaveners in this recipe, it is important to beat the mixture for the full amount of time to incorporate air into the batter.
- Using a rubber spatula, gently stir the dry ingredients into the chocolate mixture until fully incorporated and no traces of flour remain.
- Pour the batter into the prepared pan and spread evenly over the bottom and into the corners.
- Bake for 48 to 55 minutes or until a toothpick inserted into the center comes out mostly clean.
- Allow to cool in pan for 20 minutes. Using the parchment paper as handles, gently lift the brownies from the pan and place on a rack to cool.
- Store at room temperature.

Baker's note
The espresso powder is used here to intensify the flavor of the chocolate, but it does not taste like coffee.

Chapter 5
PIES AND TARTS

PIE CRUST DOUGH

This is a flaky pie crust dough that can be used for both sweet and savory pies.

You need:

2½ cups all-purpose flour
1 teaspoon salt
1 tablespoon granulated
  sugar
1 cup cold unsalted butter,
  cut into cubes
¼ to ½ cup ice water

Preparation:

- Place the flour, salt, and sugar in the bowl of a food processor, and pulse for a few seconds to combine.
- Add the cubed, cold butter, and pulse until the butter is about the size of peas and the mixture is sandy, about 10 pulses.
- With the machine running, add the ice water in a slow, steady stream through the feed tube, just until the dough comes together—not all the water may be used. As soon as the dough starts to pull away from the sides, stop processing. This happens very quickly. The mixture may be a tad crumbly with specks of cold butter throughout. This is what you want.
- Turn the dough out onto a clean surface and divide in half. Wrap each piece tightly with plastic wrap and flatten to form a disks.
- Refrigerate for at least 1 hour before using, or freeze for up to 3 months, making sure dough is well wrapped.
- If frozen, thaw before using.

Makes two 9-inch crusts.

BUTTERMILK PECAN PIE

I adapted this recipe from my aunt Leticia, who has been making this pie at Thanksgiving for as many years as I can remember.

You need:

1 pie crust
½ unsalted butter, melted
1⅓ cups granulated sugar
3 large eggs
3 tablespoons all-purpose flour
¼ teaspoon salt
1 cup buttermilk
2 teaspoons vanilla extract
1½ cups pecans

Preparation:

- Preheat oven to 350°F.

FOR THE CRUST:
- Roll out pie crust just slightly larger than your pie plate.
- Gently fit the dough into a 9-inch deep dish pie plate, being careful not to stretch the dough. Trim off any excess dough, then tuck the edges under and crimp the border. Put the pie plate and crust into the refrigerator to chill while you make the filling.

FOR THE FILLING:
- In a large bowl, combine melted butter and sugar. Whisk to combine.
- Add the eggs one at a time, mixing well after each addition.
- Add the flour and salt and whisk until just incorporated.
- Whisk in the buttermilk and vanilla.
- Place your chilled pie plate and crust onto a rimmed baking sheet.
- Place the pecans in the bottom of your crust. Pour the buttermilk mixture carefully over the pecans.
- Bake for 65 to 70 minutes until golden brown and slightly puffed in the center.
- Allow pie to set and cool completely. Serve chilled or at room temperature.
- Cover and refrigerate any leftovers.

Baker's note
When baking pies with gooey fillings, it is a good idea to place a rimmed baking sheet lined with parchment paper under the pie to catch any drips or overflows that may occur during the baking process. It also makes cleanup easier.

CHOCOLATE ANGEL PIE

This pie is so light and ethereal. This meringue crust is reminiscent of toasted marshmallows.

You need:

MERINGUE CRUST:
3 large egg whites
⅛ teaspoon salt
⅛ teaspoon cream of tartar
½ cup granulated sugar

CHOCOLATE MOUSSE FILLING:
- 3 tablespoons milk
- 6 ounces semisweet chocolate, chopped
- 1½ cups heavy cream
- ½ teaspoon vanilla extract

Preparation:

FOR THE CRUST:
- Preheat oven to 300°F.
- Lightly butter a 9-inch pie plate and set aside.
- In a large bowl, beat egg whites, salt, and cream of tartar with an electric mixer on medium-high speed until foamy. With the mixer still running, gradually add the sugar a couple tablespoons at a time until it is fully incorporated.
- Continue to whip the egg whites until glossy and stiff peaks form. It's ready when it's silky but still holds its shape.
- Pile the meringue into the center of the pie plate. Push the meringue out to the edges, building up the sides to form a crust.
- Bake for 50 to 55 minutes until the meringue is evenly toasted and set.
- Allow the crust to cool while you make the filling.

FOR THE FILLING:
- Place chocolate in a medium bowl and set aside.
- Heat milk in a small bowl in the microwave until hot and steamy, but not boiling. Pour the milk over the chocolate and let it sit for a couple minutes. Stir the chocolate until it is completely melted and smooth. Let mixture cool.
- In a medium bowl, whip the heavy cream and vanilla to the soft peak stage. If you over whip the cream, your mousse will be grainy. Soft, creamy, and pillowy is the texture you're looking for.
- Once the cream has been whipped, fold the cream into the cooled chocolate, a little at a time until fully incorporated and no white streaks remain.
- Immediately scrape the filling into the cooled meringue shell, smoothing the top.
- Cover loosely and refrigerate at least 2 hours or overnight before serving.

CHOCOLATE PEANUT BUTTER MOUSSE PIE

I've never been a big fan of chocolate and peanut butter together, but my older brother, Joseph, loves the combination. This pie is dedicated to him and all the chocolate peanut butter lovers of the world.

You need:

CHOCOLATE COOKIE CRUST:

1½ cups chocolate cookie crumbs

5 tablespoons unsalted butter, melted

PEANUT BUTTER MOUSSE:

1¼ cups heavy cream

2½ ounces cream cheese, room temperature

1 tablespoon unsalted butter, room temperature

⅔ cup powdered sugar

⅓ cup creamy peanut butter

CHOCOLATE MOUSSE:

5 ounces semisweet chocolate, coarsely chopped

3 tablespoons milk

3 tablespoons granulated sugar

½ teaspoon vanilla extract

CHOCOLATE GANACHE:

3 ounces semisweet chocolate, finely chopped

⅓ cup heavy cream

½ teaspoon vanilla extract

peanuts for garnish, optional

Preparation:

FOR THE CRUST:
- In a medium bowl, stir together the cookie crumbs and the melted butter. Stir until well combined.
- Pat the mixture into the bottom and up the sides of a 9-inch deep dish pie plate.
- Refrigerate the crust while you make the peanut butter mousse.

FOR THE PEANUT BUTTER MOUSSE:
- In a large, clean bowl, beat the heavy cream with an electric mixer at high speed until soft peaks form. Set aside.
- In a large bowl using an electric mixer, beat the cream cheese and butter at medium speed until creamy. Add the powdered sugar and mix until well blended. Add the peanut butter and mix until well blended, scraping down the sides of the bowl as necessary.
- Gently fold ½ cup of the whipped cream into the peanut butter mixture until almost blended. Fold in another ¾ cup of the whipped cream until completely blended and no white streaks appear.
- Scrape the peanut butter mousse into the chilled crust and spread it into an even layer.
- Refrigerate the pie while you make the chocolate mousse. Cover the remaining whipped cream and refrigerate until ready to use.

FOR THE CHOCOLATE MOUSSE:
- Place chocolate in the bowl of a food processor and process until finely ground. Leave the chocolate in the food processor.
- In a small saucepan, combine the milk and sugar and bring to a boil over medium heat, stirring frequently until the sugar dissolves.
- With the food processor running, pour the hot milk through the feed tube, and process until the chocolate is completely melted. Scrape down the sides of the bowl, add the vanilla extract and process until well blended.
- Scrape the mixture into a medium bowl. Cool to room temperature if warm.
- Using a rubber spatula, gently fold one-quarter of the reserved whipped cream into the chocolate. Fold in the remaining cream until completely blended.
- Scrape the chocolate mousse on top of the peanut butter mousse layer and smooth the top. Refrigerate the pie while making the chocolate ganache.

Continued…

CHOCOLATE PEANUT BUTTER MOUSSE PIE

FOR THE CHOCOLATE GANACHE:

- Place finely chopped chocolate into a small bowl.
- In a small saucepan, heat the cream until hot and steamy but not boiling. Pour cream over the chocolate and let sit for a few minutes.
- Add the vanilla, then gently stir until the chocolate is completely melted and smooth. Do not whisk or you'll incorporate air bubbles. Let the mixture cool at room temperature for 5 to 10 minutes before using. It will thicken slightly as it sits.
- Pour the cooled ganache over the top of the pie. Spread it evenly over the top of the pie.
- Sprinkle a handful of peanuts over the ganache before it sets.
- Cover loosely and refrigerate at least two hours or overnight before serving.

COCONUT KEY LIME PIE

When I was expecting my son, I had constant cravings for tangy key lime pie. This is one of my favorites updated with a slightly chewy coconut crust and brown sugar whipped cream.

You need:

COCONUT GRAHAM CRUST:
1¼ cups graham cracker crumbs
¼ cup shredded coconut
2 tablespoons brown sugar, packed
6 tablespoons unsalted butter, melted

KEY LIME FILLING:
14 ounces sweetened condensed milk
3 large egg yolks
½ cup key lime juice
1 teaspoon finely grated lime zest

BROWN SUGAR WHIPPED CREAM:
½ cup heavy cream
2 teaspoons light brown sugar
½ teaspoon vanilla

GARNISH:
¼ cup toasted coconut
Fresh limes wedges

Preparation:

FOR THE CRUST:
- Preheat oven to 350°F.
- In a medium bowl, combine graham cracker crumbs, coconut, and sugar. Stir in the melted butter until thoroughly blended.
- Press mixture firmly into a 9-inch pie pan and press firmly to bottom and sides, bringing crumbs evenly up to the rim.
- Bake for 8 to 10 minutes. While the crust is baking, toast the coconut.

TO TOAST THE COCONUT:
- Place ¼ cup shredded coconut in a thin layer on a sheet pan. Bake in the oven along the pie crust for 8 to 10 minutes, stirring once halfway through the baking time, until coconut is evenly browned.
- Place the graham crust on a rack and allow to cool while you make the filling. Allow the coconut to cool on the sheet pan.

FOR THE FILLING:
- Combine condensed milk, egg yolks, lime juice, and zest in a medium bowl. Blend until smooth, then pour filling into graham cracker crust.
- Bake for 15 minutes.
- Allow to cool for 20 minutes before refrigerating. Refrigerate until completely chilled.

FOR THE TOPPING:
- In a medium bowl, combine heavy cream, brown sugar, and vanilla. Beat with an electric mixer at medium speed until the cream is stiff enough to hold its shape. Do not overbeat.
- Pipe whipped cream around the outer edge of your pie, then sprinkle the toasted coconut over the cream and decorate with fresh lime wedges.
- Store pie loosely covered in the refrigerator.

LEMON SHORTBREAD TART

Pucker up! This tart is loaded with vibrant lemon flavor.

You need:

SHORTBREAD CRUST:
2 cups all-purpose flour
½ cup granulated sugar
¼ teaspoon salt
½ cup cold unsalted butter, cut into cubes
1 large egg, lightly beaten

LEMON FILLING:
½ cup all-purpose flour
1 cup granulated sugar
4 large eggs
3 tablespoons finely grated lemon zest
¾ cup fresh lemon juice

GARNISH:
A dusting of powdered sugar

Preparation:

FOR THE CRUST:
- Preheat oven to 350°F.
- In a large bowl, combine the flour, sugar, and salt. Whisk to combine.
- Using a pastry cutter, cut the cold cubed butter into the dry ingredients until the butter is uniformly blended into the flour mixture.
- Stir the egg into the flour mixture until it resembles sand and holds together when squeezed between the palm of your hand.
- Place the crumbly mixture into an 11-inch tart pan and press the dough firmly into the bottom and the sides forming a crust.
- Place the tart pan on a baking sheet and place in the refrigerator to chill until the crust firms up, about 10 to 15 minutes.
- Bake for 15 minutes.
- While the crust is baking, make the filling.

FOR THE FILLING:
- In a medium bowl, whisk the flour, sugar, and eggs together until combined. Stir in the lemon zest and juice and whisk until well blended.
- When the crust is done baking, pour the lemon filling into the hot crust and carefully return it back to the oven.
- Bake for an additional 25 minutes or until the center of the tart is set.
- Cool to room temperature, then chill for at least two hours or overnight.
- Dust with powdered sugar just before serving.
- Store leftovers in the tart pan, loosely covered in the refrigerator.

Makes one 11-inch tart.

PINEAPPLE COCONUT CHESS PIE

I dedicate this pie to my late grandfather-in-law, HAH. I never had the honor of meeting him, but this was his favorite pie.

You need:

1 pie crust
½ cup unsalted butter, melted
1½ cups granulated sugar
1 tablespoon cornmeal
1 tablespoon all-purpose flour
⅛ teaspoon salt
½ teaspoon vanilla extract
4 large eggs
2 cups shredded coconut
8 ounces crushed pineapple, drained

Preparation:

- Preheat oven to 350°F.

FOR THE CRUST:
- Roll out pie crust just slightly larger than your pie plate.
- Gently fit the dough into a 9-inch deep dish pie plate, being careful not to stretch the dough. Trim off any excess dough, then tuck the edges under and crimp the border. Put the pie plate and crust into the refrigerator to chill while you make the filling.

FOR THE FILLING:
- In a large bowl, combine the butter, sugar, cornmeal, flour, salt, and vanilla. Whisk together until well blended.
- Add the eggs, one at a time, whisking well after each addition.
- Stir the coconut and pineapple into the egg mixture.
- Pour the filling into the chilled crust.
- Bake for 55 to 60 minutes or until the center of the pie has set.
- Cool to room temperature then chill for at least 2 hours or overnight.
- Serve chilled or at room temperature.

CHOCOLATE-SALTED CARAMEL PRETZEL TART

This tart combines sweet and salty in the best way possible. The soft caramel filling, the rich chocolate, and the crunchy crust taste like you're eating a chocolate toffee bar.

You need:

PRETZEL CRUST:
1¾ cups finely crushed pretzels
⅓ cup granulated sugar
¾ cup unsalted butter, melted

SALTED CARAMEL:
1¼ cups granulated sugar
½ cup cold salted butter, cut into cubes
¾ cup heavy cream, room temperature
½ teaspoon sea salt
½ teaspoon vanilla extract

CHOCOLATE GANACHE:
1¼ cups heavy cream
1½ cups semisweet chocolate chips

Preparation:

FOR THE CRUST:
- In a medium bowl, combine pretzel crumbs and sugar. Stir in the melted butter until thoroughly blended.
- Place the mixture into an 11-inch tart pan and press the crumbs firmly into the bottom and up the sides forming a crust.
- Place the tart pan on a baking sheet and place in the oven.
- Bake for 14 minutes.

FOR THE CARAMEL:
- Place the sugar in a heavy-bottomed 3-quart pot and cook over medium-high heat. Whisk the sugar as it melts. Continue to whisk as it cooks and turns into a deep amber-colored syrup.
- Add the butter to the hot, melted sugar and stir until melted.
- As you pour in the heavy cream, the mixture will bubble and foam. Be careful not to burn yourself. Whisk constantly until you have a smooth sauce.
- Remove the pan from the heat, stir in the sea salt and vanilla. Let the mixture cool to room temperature until thickened, but is still pourable.
- Pour the caramel into the baked and cooled pretzel crust. Let cool in the refrigerator until caramel is firm.

FOR THE GANACHE:
- Place the chocolate in a small mixing bowl.
- In a small saucepan, heat the cream until hot and steamy but not boiling. Pour cream over the chocolate and let it rest for a few minutes.
- Gently stir the chocolate until it is completely melted and smooth. Do not whisk or you'll incorporate air bubbles. Let the mixture cool to room temperature for about 10 minutes before using. It will thicken slightly as it sits.
- Pour the cooled ganache over the top of the caramel. Garnish with pretzels before the ganache sets.
- Place the tart back into the refrigerator until firm. Serve chilled.
- Store leftovers in the tart pan, loosely covered in the refrigerator.

Makes one 11-inch tart.

Baker's note
This tart is sticky and gooey. If you try to slice it at room temperature, the caramel will ooze out all over the place. It is best to keep it well chilled and cut it with a sharp knife, wiping down the blade after each cut.

Chapter 6

PUDDINGS AND CREAMS

BERRIES ROMANOFF

You need:

6 cups assorted fresh berries, rinsed and patted dry
1 cup sour cream
⅓ cup brown sugar, packed
1 tablespoon brandy liquor

Preparation:

- In a small mixing bowl, combine sour cream, brown sugar, and brandy. Whisk together until a pourable consistency.
- Divide your berries evenly between 6 small bowls or cups. Evenly divide the sour cream sauce over the berries.

Serves 6.

CRANBERRY FREEZE

My mother-in-law has been making this frozen dessert for as long as I've known her. The holidays just aren't the same without it.

You need:

8 ounces cream cheese, room temperature

2 tablespoons granulated sugar

2 tablespoons mayonnaise

8 ounces sour cream

2 cups whole berry cranberry sauce, homemade or canned

8 ounces crushed pineapple in juice

½ cup chopped pecans

12 ounces Cool Whip, thawed

Preparation:

- Line a 9 × 13-inch dish with parchment paper, leaving the ends long enough to hang over the sides. Set aside.
- In a large bowl, blend cream cheese and sugar with an electric mixer on medium speed until creamy. Add the mayonnaise and sour cream and mix well.
- Add the cranberry sauce, pineapple, and pecans and stir until fully incorporated.
- Using a large rubber spatula, fold in the softened cool whip until well blended.
- Pour the cranberry mixture into the parchment lined dish and freeze until completely solid.
- Allow frozen dessert to sit at room temperature for 5 to 10 minutes. Cut into squares and serve. Add Cool Whip as topping as desired.
- Cranberry freeze will keep for 3 months, well wrapped in the freezer.

Baker's note
For individual servings of cranberry freeze, line muffin tins with paper liners and lightly spray them with nonstick cooking spray. Fill the cups to the top with the cranberry mixture and freeze. Peel off the paper before serving.

NUTELLA PANNA COTTA

Panna cotta is an Italian dessert of cooked cream and sugar that is set with gelatin. It is similar to pudding, but does not contain any eggs. This version incorporates chocolate and Nutella to make it even richer.

You need:

1 envelope (2¼ teaspoons) powdered gelatin
3 tablespoons cold water
1½ cups heavy cream
⅛ teaspoon salt
¼ cup semisweet chocolate chips
1 cup Nutella
1 teaspoon vanilla extract
1 cup milk

Preparation:

- Lightly butter 6 small cups or ramekins. Place them on a rimmed baking sheet and set aside.
- Place a sieve over a large measuring cup with spout and set aside.
- Place cold water in a small bowl and sprinkle the gelatin over the surface of the water. Let it rest for 5 minutes. Do not stir.
- In a medium saucepan, combine cream, salt, and chocolate chips. Stirring constantly over medium-high heat, melt the chocolate and bring the cream to a boil.
- Add the gelatin mixture to the hot cream and whisk until dissolved.
- Remove the pan from the heat and whisk in the Nutella and vanilla. Once creamy and smooth, stir in the milk until well combined.
- Strain the mixture through a sieve into the measuring cup.
- Carefully pour the Nutella cream into the buttered ramekins, evenly dividing the mixture as you pour.
- Place the baking sheet of ramekins into the refrigerator and chill for 2 to 3 hours or until set.
- Invert the chilled puddings or enjoy them right out of the cups.
- Store in the refrigerator wrapped with plastic wrap for up to 3 days.

Serves 6.

BROWN SUGAR SOUR CREAM PANNA COTTA

This panna cotta is creamy and decadent. Serving it with tart berries will help break up the richness.

You need:

1 envelope (2¼ teaspoons) powdered gelatin
2 tablespoons cold water
2 cups heavy cream
1 cup brown sugar, packed
½ cup sour cream
2 tablespoons brandy liquor, optional
½ teaspoon vanilla extract
Fresh berries for garnish

Preparation:

- Lightly butter 6 small cups or ramekins. Place them on a rimmed baking sheet and set aside.
- Place a sieve over a large measuring cup with spout and set aside.
- Place cold water in a small bowl and sprinkle the gelatin over the surface of the water. Let it rest for 5 minutes. Do not stir.
- In a medium saucepan, combine cream and brown sugar. Stir constantly over medium-high heat until the sugar dissolves and the mixture comes to a boil.
- Add the gelatin mixture to the hot cream and whisk until dissolved.
- Remove the pan from the heat and whisk in the sour cream, brandy, and vanilla until creamy and smooth.
- Strain the mixture through a sieve into the measuring cup.
- Carefully pour the cream mixture into the buttered ramekins, evenly dividing the mixture as you pour.
- Place the baking sheet of ramekins into the refrigerator and chill for 2 to 3 hours or until set.
- Serve in the ramekins with fresh berries.
- Store in the refrigerator wrapped with plastic wrap for up to 3 days.

Serves 6.

Baker's note

The brandy liquor is an optional ingredient.
If you prefer not to use it, just omit it and
increase the vanilla extract to 1 teaspoon.

CREAMY RICE PUDDING

Sometimes you just need a bowl of comforting rice pudding and nothing else will do.

You need:

½ cup arborio rice, uncooked
2½ cups milk
1½ cups heavy cream
⅓ cup granulated sugar
1 cinnamon stick
½ vanilla bean, split
    and scraped

Preparation:

- In a 3-quart, heavy-bottomed saucepan, combine all the ingredients and stir together.
- Cook over medium-high heat and bring to a boil.
- Reduce the heat to low and simmer for 40 to 45 minutes, stirring often until rice is tender and creamy.
- Continue to stir as the mixture thickens to prevent sticking.
- Carefully remove the cinnamon stick and vanilla bean and discard.
- Serve warm, room temperature, or chilled.
- Store in the refrigerator for up to a week.

Serves 4.

Baker's note

If you don't have a vanilla bean, you can substitute with 1 teaspoon vanilla extract. After the rice has been thoroughly cooked, stir in extract then serve.

TIRAMISU

You need:

1 cup brewed espresso, cooled
2 tablespoons coffee liqueur
2 large egg yolks
1/3 cup granulated sugar
8 ounces mascarpone cheese,
    room temperature
1/4 teaspoon salt
2 tablespoons dark rum
3/4 cup heavy cream
24 ladyfingers
2 tablespoons unsweetened
    cocoa powder

Preparation:

- Place cooled espresso and coffee liqueur in a shallow dish and mix to combine. Set aside.
- In a large bowl, beat egg yolks with an electric mixer on medium speed until slightly foamy. Add the sugar and beat until light in color and thickened, about 2 to 3 minutes.
- Add the softened mascarpone cheese, salt, and rum and beat until well combined and creamy. Set aside.
- In a medium bowl, beat the heavy cream until it has doubled in volume and soft peaks form. Stir one-third of the whipped cream into the cheese mixture. Then gently fold the remaining cream into the cheese mixture until fully incorporated. Set aside.
- Quickly dip the ladyfingers, one at a time, into the coffee mixture. This should take no longer than 2 to 3 seconds per ladyfinger. Place them side by side in a single layer in the bottom of a 9 x 9-inch baking dish. If you need to break them to fit into the dish, this is okay, just face them all in the same direction.
- Spread half of the mascarpone mixture in an even layer over the coffee soaked ladyfingers. Smooth the top and dust with 1 tablespoon of cocoa.
- Repeat this process with the remaining ladyfingers. Spread the cheese mixture evenly over the ladyfingers and smooth the top of the surface. Evenly dust the top with the remaining tablespoon of cocoa powder.
- Cover and refrigerate for 4 hours or overnight.

Serves 9

Baker's note
You can use full-fat cream cheese in place of the mascarpone cheese, if you have trouble finding it.

Chapter 7
BREAKFAST SWEETS

BLUEBERRY ORANGE CRUMB CAKE

A light, moist cake bursting with orange zest and blueberries. Perfect for lazy Saturday mornings.

You need:

CRUMBS:

1 cup all-purpose flour
½ cup brown sugar, packed
⅛ teaspoon salt
½ teaspoon ground cinnamon
½ cup cold unsalted butter, cut into cubes

BLUEBERRY ORANGE CAKE:

1¾ cups all-purpose flour
2 teaspoons baking powder
¼ teaspoon salt
½ cup unsalted butter, room temperature
1 cup granulated sugar
1 large egg
1 tablespoon finely grated orange zest
½ teaspoon vanilla extract
⅔ cup buttermilk
1½ cups blueberries

Preparation:

- Preheat oven to 375°F.
- Butter an 8 × 8-inch baking dish and set aside.

FOR THE CRUMB MIXTURE:

- In a large bowl, combine the flour, sugar, salt, and cinnamon. Whisk to combine.
- Using a pastry cutter, cut the cold cubed butter into the dry ingredients until the butter is uniformly blended into the flour mixture and is moist and sandy. Take the mixture in your hand and squeeze to form several large crumbs.
- Place the bowl in the refrigerator while you prepare the batter for the cake.

FOR THE CAKE:

- In a medium bowl, combine the flour, baking powder, and salt. Whisk to combine and set aside.
- In a large bowl, beat the butter, and sugar together until light and fluffy.
- Add the egg, orange zest and vanilla. Stir to combine.
- Add half of the dry ingredients to the butter mixture and blend until just combined, then add in all of the buttermilk, followed by the remaining flour and mix, just until incorporated.
- Using a rubber spatula, gently fold the blueberries into the batter.
- Scrape the batter into the prepared pan and smooth the top.
- Gently break up the large crumbs and scatter the mixture evenly over the cake.
- Bake for 40 to 45 minutes or until a toothpick inserted into the center comes out clean.
- Cool before serving.
- Store at room temperature.

BUTTERMILK SPICE MUFFINS

You need:

BUTTERMILK MUFFINS:

1½ cups all-purpose flour
1½ teaspoon baking powder
½ teaspoon baking soda
½ teaspoon salt
½ teaspoon freshly
   grated nutmeg
½ cup unsalted butter, room
   temperature
¾ cup granulated sugar
1 large egg
1 teaspoon vanilla extract
⅔ cup buttermilk

SPICE TOPPING:

½ cup granulated sugar
2 teaspoons ground cinnamon
½ teaspoon freshly
   ground nutmeg
¼ cup unsalted butter, melted

Preparation:

FOR THE MUFFINS:

- Preheat an oven to 350°F.
- Line standard muffin tins with 12 paper liners or spray with nonstick baking spray and set aside.
- In a small bowl, stir together the flour, baking powder, baking soda, salt, and nutmeg.
- In a large bowl, combine the butter and sugar and beat with an electric mixer on medium speed until light and fluffy. Add the egg and vanilla and beat well.
- Add half of the dry ingredients to the butter mixture and blend until just combined.
- Add in all of the buttermilk, followed by the remaining flour, and mix just until incorporated and no traces of flour remain, but do not overmix.
- Evenly divide the batter between the paper liners.
- Bake for 20 to 25 minutes, or until a toothpick inserted into the center comes out clean.
- Allow to cool for 5 minutes in the pan, then place them on a rack to cool while you make the topping.

FOR THE TOPPING:

- In a small bowl, combine the sugar, cinnamon, and nutmeg. Stir to combine. Put the melted butter in another small bowl.
- Just as soon as the muffins are cool enough to handle, but are still warm, hold the bottom part of the muffins and dip the top into the melted butter, gently turning to coat it evenly.
- Immediately dip the buttered muffin tops into the spiced sugar mixture, coating it evenly.
- Return the muffins, right side up, to the cooling rack. Repeat until all the muffins have been buttered and sugared.
- Serve warm or at room temperature.

Makes 12 muffins.

SOUR CREAM COFFEE CAKE

A truly simple cake that is perfect for all occasions. It doesn't look like much, but believe me when I say it is addicting.

You need:

STREUSEL:

¼ cup granulated sugar
¾ cup plus 2 tablespoons all-purpose flour
½ cup cold, unsalted butter, cut into cubes

SOUR CREAM CAKE:

1¼ cups sour cream
1¼ teaspoons baking soda
⅛ teaspoon salt
½ cup unsalted butter, room temperature
1¼ cups granulated sugar
2 large eggs
1 teaspoon vanilla extract
1¾ cups all-purpose flour
1¾ teaspoons baking powder

Preparation:

- Preheat the oven to 350°F.
- Butter a 9 × 13-inch baking dish and set aside.

FOR THE STREUSEL TOPPING:

- In a small bowl, combine the sugar and flour. Whisk to combine then add the cubed butter.
- Using a pastry cutter, cut the cold cubed butter into the dry ingredients until the butter is uniformly blended into the flour mixture and is a moist sandy consistency. Take the streusel in your hand and squeeze the mixture to form several large pieces.
- Place in refrigerator while you make the cake.

FOR THE CAKE:

- Place the sour cream in a small bowl and sift the baking soda and salt into it. Stir to blend evenly and set aside. As the sour cream mixture sits, it will get airy.
- In a large bowl, beat the butter, sugar, eggs, and vanilla together with an electric mixer on medium speed until light and fluffy.
- Sift the flour and baking powder over the top of the butter mixture and stir.
- Add the sour cream mixture and stir until just combined.
- Scrape the batter into the prepared dish and smooth the surface.
- Gently break up the large crumbs and scatter the mixture evenly over the cake.
- Bake for 40 to 45 minutes or until a toothpick inserted into the center comes out clean.
- Cool slightly. Serve warm or at room temperature.
- Store at room temperature.

CRANBERRY ORANGE BREAD

This is one of the lightest and tastiest quick breads. I've made it into muffins and mini loaves before, but my favorite way to enjoy it is to cut a thick slice, warm it, and serve with a pat of butter.

You need:

2 cups all-purpose flour

1½ teaspoons baking powder

½ teaspoon baking soda

1 teaspoon salt

3 tablespoons unsalted butter, room temperature

1 cup granulated sugar

1 tablespoon finely grated orange zest

1 large egg

¾ cup fresh orange juice

1½ cups fresh or frozen cranberries, roughly chopped

Preparation:

- Preheat oven to 350°F.
- Grease a 9 × 5-inch loaf pan with nonstick baking spray and set aside.
- In a medium bowl, combine flour, baking powder, baking soda, and salt. Whisk to combine and set aside.
- In a large bowl, cream butter and sugar together using a hand mixer at medium speed. Add the orange zest and egg. Mix until well combined and fluffy.
- Add half of the flour mixture to the butter mixture and mix until just combined. Stir in the orange juice, mix until just incorporated, then add the remaining flour and mix once again until no white streaks of flour remain.
- Using a rubber spatula, stir in chopped cranberries. Spread evenly into prepared loaf pan.
- Bake for 55 to 60 minutes or until a toothpick inserted in the center comes out clean. Cool on a rack for 15 minutes. Remove from pan. Cool completely. Wrap and store overnight.

Makes 1 loaf.

Baker's note

You don't have to wrap and store this overnight, but doing so allows the flavors to meld together. It just gets better by the day.

BANANA PECAN BREAKFAST CAKE

When I was putting together recipes for this cookbook, I knew I had to include something with bananas and cinnamon for my friend Ingrid and her kids. We got to know each other through our blogs, but it was our passion for baking and our bond as mothers that has kept us close. I'm certain they'd devour this cake straight out of the oven.

You need:

BANANA CAKE:

1½ cups all-purpose flour
¾ teaspoons baking powder
¾ teaspoons baking soda
½ teaspoon salt
½ teaspoon ground cinnamon
½ cup unsalted butter,
   room temperature
¾ cup granulated sugar
1 large egg
1 teaspoon vanilla extract
1 cup mashed ripe bananas
¼ cup buttermilk

PECAN TOPPING:

¼ cup brown sugar, packed
⅓ cup chopped pecans
½ teaspoon ground cinnamon

Preparation:

FOR THE CAKE:

- Preheat oven to 350°F.
- Grease an 8 × 8-inch baking pan with nonstick baking spray and set aside.
- In a medium bowl, combine the flour, baking powder, baking soda, salt, and cinnamon. Whisk to combine and set aside.
- In a large bowl, cream the butter and sugar together with an electric mixer at medium speed until light and fluffy.
- Add the egg, vanilla, and mashed bananas and blend until incorporated.
- Add half of the flour mixture to the banana mixture and mix until just combined. Stir in all of the buttermilk and mix until just incorporated, then add the remaining flour and mix once again until no traces of flour remain.
- Scrape the batter into the prepared baking dish and smooth the top.

FOR THE TOPPING:

- Combine the sugar, pecans, and cinnamon in a small bowl. Stir together, then evenly sprinkle the mixture over the cake batter.
- Bake for 40 to 45 minutes or until a toothpick inserted in the center comes out clean.
- Cool slightly. Serve warm or at room temperature.
- Store at room temperature.

ACKNOWLEDGMENTS

Thank you to my husband, Sam, for supporting and encouraging me every step of the way. For indulging me while I talked on and on about recipe concepts and for making grocery store runs at midnight when I ran out of heavy cream. Thank you for being my photo assistant, cleaning up after me and eating frozen meals when I was too tired to cook. I love you.

To my little love, Hayden, for being a Junior baker and helping me in the kitchen. I needed your little hands to turn on and off the stand mixer, to stir dry ingredients, to pour milk into batters and to turn on and off the oven (sometimes before the timer went off). You are a champion test taster and sampled every step of the way.

To my mom, Laura, for helping any way you could. Thank you for being a dishwasher, a babysitter, a grocery shopper, a prop supplier and for offering your honest opinion about my not-so-successful recipe blunders. Thank you for always being there for me and believing in me even when I didn't.

To my Grandma, Diana, for giving me my very first cookbook and introducing me to baking. You are and always will be my number one fan.

To my mother-in-law, Nonie, for contributing recipes, ideas, and for letting me raid through your china cabinets and kitchen for linens and props. Thank you for keeping me in constant supply of shelled homegrown pecans and for willingly eating all my unsuccessful attempts at pies, cakes and bars.

To my brother Aaron for making last minute store runs and for listening to me complain when I became frustrated.

To my aunt Letty for contributing your buttermilk pecan pie recipe.

To my great aunt Mary for passing down your recipe for sugar cookies.

To my neighbors, Jim and Andrea, for your amazing pecan butter balls recipe.

To Ingrid for recipe testing and offering suggestions on how to make them better.

To Heather for letting me use your peanut butter cookie recipe and for meeting me for coffee breaks at Starbucks.

To all my friends and family who have willingly sampled my baking experiments and for supporting me each and every step of the way. I couldn't have done this without you!

To Kristin Kulsavage at Skyhorse Publishing for being a fan of my blog, for reaching out to me and offering me this opportunity to write a cookbook. Thank you for having faith in my abilities as a writer and a self taught baker. Thank you, thank you, thank you for turning my dream into a reality.

INDEX

METRIC AND IMPERIAL CONVERSIONS

(These conversions are rounded for convenience)

Ingredient	Cups/Tablespoons/Teaspoons	Ounces	Grams/Milliliters
Butter	1 cup=16 tablespoons= 2 sticks	8 ounces	230 grams
Cream cheese	1 tablespoon	0.5 ounce	14.5 grams
Cheese, shredded	1 cup	4 ounces	110 grams
Cornstarch	1 tablespoon	0.3 ounce	8 grams
Flour, all-purpose	1 cup/1 tablespoon	4.5 ounces/0.3 ounce	125 grams/8 grams
Flour, whole wheat	1 cup	4 ounces	120 grams
Fruit, dried	1 cup	4 ounces	120 grams
Fruits or veggies, chopped	1 cup	5 to 7 ounces	145 to 200 grams
Fruits or veggies, puréed	1 cup	8.5 ounces	245 grams
Honey, maple syrup, or corn syrup	1 tablespoon	.75 ounce	20 grams
Liquids: cream, milk, water, or juice	1 cup	8 fluid ounces	240 milliliters
Oats	1 cup	5.5 ounces	150 grams
Salt	1 teaspoon	0.2 ounces	6 grams
Spices: cinnamon, cloves, ginger, or nutmeg (ground)	1 teaspoon	0.2 ounce	5 milliliters
Sugar, brown, firmly packed	1 cup	7 ounces	200 grams
Sugar, white	1 cup/1 tablespoon	7 ounces/0.5 ounce	200 grams/12.5 grams
Vanilla extract	1 teaspoon	0.2 ounce	4 grams

OVEN TEMPERATURES

Fahrenheit	Celcius	Gas Mark
225°	110°	¼
250°	120°	½
275°	140°	1
300°	150°	2
325°	160°	3
350°	180°	4
375°	190°	5
400°	200°	6
425°	220°	7
450°	230°	8

BAKING NOTES

_____
_____
_____
_____
_____
_____
_____
_____
_____
_____
_____
_____
_____
_____
_____
_____
_____
_____
_____
_____
_____
_____
_____
_____
_____
_____